HEALING IN THE SPIRIT

Jim McManus, C.Ss.R.

HEALING
IN THE SPIRIT

*Inner Healing and Deliverance
in Today's Church*

DARTON · LONGMAN + TODD

First published 1994 by
Darton, Longman and Todd Ltd
1 Spencer Court
140–142 Wandsworth High Street
London SW18 4JJ

ISBN 0–232–52093–3

A catalogue record for this book is available from the
British Library

Biblical quotations are taken from *The New Jerusalem Bible*
published and copyright 1985 by
Darton, Longman and Todd Ltd and Doubleday and Co. Inc.

Phototypeset in 10½/13pt Plantin by Intype, London
Printed and bound in Great Britain by
Page Bros, Norwich

To my five brothers and three sisters,
in gratitude for life-long love and support.

Contents

Foreword

There is increasing interest in the ministry of healing but most people still hold back because they are unsure how to begin and have the impression that healing was only common in the early years of the Church and is now confined to 'special' people. Those who hesitate will find much encouragement in this book and once they have begun they will want to read on. Father Jim McManus leads us along his own path of spiritual discovery as he shares with us some of his pastoral experiences and the insights he has gained. All that he has come to understand is clearly supported by the Scriptures and the texts of the Second Vatican Council, and he helps us to see these with new eyes.

Healing was integral to Christ's ministry and was continued by the apostles as the Holy Spirit worked in them as he had in Christ. Healing spearheaded evangelization by the early Christians but when it declined after the time of Constantine the theory was propounded that it was a special gift for the beginning of the Church. Now a renewed understanding of the sacraments and especially those of reconciliation and anointing of the sick makes it clear that healing is a central work of the Church as it was of Christ. Nor is it limited to the ordained ministers because we know that the Holy Spirit works in all members of the Church and Christ promised that we are to do the same works as he did himself and indeed greater works.

It is always Christ who heals and his healing involves the whole person. The fullness of life which is Christ's wish for us is only possible if we are able to accept ourselves as Christ made us and are convinced that we are truly precious in his sight. This is called healing of the self-image and is the first step towards healing of our relationships with others through forgiveness and the healing of our memories through changing the way in which we remember the past. There is no question of a special technique: it is simply a matter of willingly and honestly bringing all our past hurts and resentments before Christ and asking him to heal them while giving us the power to forgive.

When inner healing does not take place in response to our prayer it is almost always because of a variety of barriers which we place in its way such as lack of self-acceptance or lack of genuine repentance. In some cases, we can be held bound by the influences of evil spirits and then there is need for prayer of deliverance which is really a command in the name of Jesus that the evil spirits should depart.

Many people think first of physical healing but this is the last topic treated in this book because it is only a very small part of the total healing ministry. Indeed it is pointed out that while someone can be healed by medical science of a serious illness and yet remain deeply embittered the physical healing brought about by Christ is always part of the total healing of the whole person. It is very often the inner spiritual healing which is the more important.

Prayer for healing with real faith can do much to enrich the celebration of the sacraments and the general ministry of Christians to one another. It was an important element in the growth of the early Church and it is urgently needed today when so many people suffer from such deep hurts. This book will convince you of its orthodoxy and give you courage to begin.

Ambrose Griffiths OSB
Bishop of Hexham and Newcastle

Introduction

During a parish mission, in a very large parish, I met a lady who had just recently lapsed from the practice of her faith. She was very angry. What she said to me then has remained with me ever since: 'The thing that hurts me most is that I am not even missed'. Nobody knew she was there, nobody knew she was not there. For the first time I got a real insight into how the faith of the individual can be at risk in a large, anonymous congregation.

This lady's bitter complaint was particularly poignant to me because I was at that time in her parish encouraging people to come back to the practice of the faith. The irony of the situation hit me between the eyes. Here I was trying to persuade her to come back to a community that did not even know she existed! I was forced to look very carefully at my own pastoral strategy. It is not sufficient to get people 'into the church'. The real challenge is to ensure that they arrive in the church as brothers and sisters, as God's family, as a true community.

Shortly after this experience I read a very significant report from the Vatican on why some Catholics leave the Church to join new religious movements. The Vatican had asked all the bishops of the Catholic world to investigate in their own dioceses why this was happening: what made these new religious movements so attractive? (As I write this I am very conscious of a telephone call that I had just yesterday. A friend rang me in great distress to inform me that twenty-five members of her once thriving prayer group had all left the Church. Some of them were eucharistic ministers and readers; all of them were devout Catholics. Now they were members of a new religious group.) In that report from the Vatican entitled *Sects: New Religious Movement?* (19 May 1986) we have a very positive analysis of this phenomenon of Catholics leaving the Church, not because they have lost their faith but because their faith is no longer nourished by their parish. Catholics are leaving the Church, we are told, because they are looking for a warm, welcoming community, in which they are known and in which their gifts are recognized and used. They are also looking for the experience of the healing love of God, touching the deep areas of their lives where they need healing. And they are looking for simple, clear, biblical answers to the complicated questions of our times.

To meet this new challenge the Holy See calls on the Church to do two things:

1   Special attention should be paid to the experiential dimension, i.e. discovering Christ personally through prayer and dedication (e.g. the charismatic and born-again movements). Many Christians live as if they had never been born at all;

2   Special attention must be given to the healing ministry through prayer, reconciliation, fellowship and care. Our pastoral concern should not be one-dimensional. It should extend not only to the spiritual, but

also to the physical, the psychological, social, cultural, economic and political dimensions.[1]

The report concludes with the observation that if we meet the challenge of the sects in this way 'the sects will prove to have been the greatest stimulus for the renewal of the Church'.

While warning us against the dangers of a 'one-dimensional ministry' the Church is emphasizing two new aspects of ministry namely 'the experiential dimension' of our faith and 'the healing ministry'. This signals a sea-change in our traditional Catholic formation in the faith. When I was being trained as a young Redemptorist I got the distinct impression, from the books I was reading, that the most dangerous thing I could ever have in my whole religious life would be a religious experience and, if I ever had such a thing, I must never speak about it to anyone. Emotions had nothing to do with spiritual and religious formation.

Today the experience of God is at the very forefront of the Church's awareness of evangelization. Pope John Paul II writes 'the evangelist is a witness to the experience of God'.[2] It is not enough to teach 'ideas about God'; nor does it even suffice to share our deepest conviction about God. There are times when we have to share our experience of God. As Jesus said to the ex-demoniac who wanted to follow him, 'Go home to your people and tell them all that the Lord in his mercy has done for you' (Mk 5.19). That is the good news. What the Lord has done for you! When you witness to that you are, in Pope John Paul's understanding of the word, an 'evangelist'.

In writing this book I have become acutely aware of the change that has taken place in my own attitude to ministry. Thirty years ago I would not have been able to approach any question of faith on the experiential level. My pastoral approach, while being based on theology, was dominated by the insights of pastoral psychology and sociology. I felt that if I really had a deep understanding of these sciences I would be well equipped for ministry.

My very first task as a priest was to teach moral theology in our seminary. I had studied moral theology in the Alphonsianum in Rome in the 1960s. It was a first-class institute. It prepared its students well for the task of teaching. But there was one area of the priest's life and work which it left untouched, that is the area of the priest's ministry as described by the Second Vatican Council: 'Priests will acquire holiness in their own distinctive way by exercising their functions sincerely and tirelessly in the Spirit of Christ' (Declaration on Priests, para 13).

What does it mean to minister in the Spirit? My theology did not tackle that subject. I had been taught well how to minister with theological and psychological insight. But there was no course on how to minister in the Spirit, with the discernment of the Spirit. There was no emphasis on the 'experiential dimension of our faith' nor on the 'healing ministry'. This is not a criticism of my theological institute. It is simply the recognition that this is a relatively new emphasis in the Catholic Church. The theology of the 1960s did not deal with this emphasis; in some cases even the theology of the 1990s is not dealing with this emphasis either.

The Holy Spirit is 'doing a new thing' in the Church. Pope John XXIII did not pray for 'a new theology'; he prayed for 'a new Pentecost'. Pope Paul VI told us 'The Church needs her perennial Pentecost: she needs fire in her heart, words on her lips, prophecy in her outlook. . . . This is what the Church needs, she needs the Holy Spirit! The

Holy Spirit in us, in each of us and in all of us together, in us who are the Church'.[3] And he reminded us that 'We are living a privileged moment of the Spirit in the Church'.[4] Pope John Paul II has continued to place the same emphasis on the Spirit. In his first encyclical he told us 'The present-day Church seems to repeat with ever greater fervour and with holy insistence: Come, Holy Spirit. . . . This appeal to the Spirit, intended precisely to obtain the Spirit, is the answer to all the materialisms of our age'.[5] There is a whole new awareness of the powerful presence of the Holy Spirit in the Church. Consequently, we can now easily talk about ministering in the Spirit and the title I am giving to this book, 'Healing in the Spirit', reflects this.

In many ways this book is a personal reflection on my own transition from a ministry over-dependent on theological and psychological insights to a ministry which seeks to be totally dependent on the Holy Spirit. As Pope Paul VI so eloquently said:

Techniques of evangelization are good, but not even the most perfect of them could replace the gentle action of the Spirit. Without the Holy Spirit, the finest preparation of the evangelist has no effect. Without him, the most convincing dialectic is powerless over the mind of man, and the most elaborate projects based on sociological or psychological data prove vain and worthless.[6]

In the first three chapters, I will outline the basic theological presuppositions of the healing ministry – the principles underlying our ministry in the Spirit. The remaining chapters show how these principles are applied in the actual ministry of healing. I try to avoid abstract discussion and illustrate the various points of teaching with examples drawn from my own pastoral experience.

In writing this book I have had the support and encouragement of many friends. My two confreres Beverly Ahearn and Tony Cassidy made many helpful suggestions. My special thanks to my editor Morag Reeve: her gentle encouragement ensured that I met the deadline.

I am especially indebted to the men and women whose stories appear in this book and in whose lives I saw the healing power of the Spirit. My thanks to each one of them, especially to Pamela, Marie and Claire who responded to my request and wrote their testimonies at short notice.

1

Our Christian Vision of the World We Live In

When I was speaking to a lady who had been diagnosed as having cancer, and given less than a year to live by her consultant, I said to her that the Lord was very close to her throughout her long illness. She replied immediately 'That is the wonder of these past months. Christ has been so close, his peace and presence so real, that I wouldn't have missed it for anything. In fact my only big worry was in case God would withdraw this wonderful peace'. Her spontaneous, faith-filled remark forced me to ask myself what kind of a perspective on life does a person have which enables her to say that she wanted this peace of Christ even more than physical health? St Paul had answered this question a long time ago: 'All I want is to know Christ and the power of his resurrection and to share his sufferings by reproducing the pattern of his death' (Phil 3.11).

It struck me vividly that here is a woman who has completely integrated her faith, not only in the way she is living the Gospel in her personal life, but in the way she is viewing everything, the whole of reality, in the light of the Gospel. Paul said 'all I want is to know Christ'; she said 'I wouldn't have missed the peace and presence of Christ for anything'.

Pamela (and I will return to her story in the last chapter

of this book) had a faith vision, or a faith-inspired perspective on her life in this world. When she looked out on our beautiful world she was aware, not just of the beauty, but of the wonderful, creative love of God which brought the whole thing into existence. Most of all, she was aware that even though she was just one minute individual in this immense cosmos, God loved her with a personal and infinite love and Christ, her Redeemer, was her closest friend. Her Christian worldview made her world appear a good and a friendly place. Despite all that is wrong, despite the terrors and the tragedies, the sickness and the struggles, God loves her world so much that 'he gave up his only-begotten to save it' (Jn 3.16). She would be the first to admit that her faith vision of life in this world was a comfort and a support to her in times of great suffering.

Not everyone, of course, has religious faith. Some years ago I was staying with very dear friends in Bavaria. The husband, an excellent person, is a convinced agnostic. On one occasion we began to discuss faith. I said that without my faith in the creative love of God, present and active in the world, the whole universe would be a very silent place. 'That's it', he responded, 'when I look at the universe I am met by utter silence'. I could look out from his lounge at the beautiful Bavarian Alps, rising majestically into the sky, and be filled with awe at God's love and power. My friend would rhapsodize about the beauty of his Alps, but could not find a whisper of God in any of them. He is a very fine man, full of kindness, goodness, patience, trustfulness – full, in fact, of many of the fruits of the Spirit (Gal 5.22). But he has no faith in God and looks out on his beautiful world, enjoying his Alps, without the slightest reference to a Creator. The great German theologian, Karl Rahner, would have seen him as 'an anonymous Christian', a man who is living the Gospel without knowing the Christ of the Gospel.

Faith Perspective

My Bavarian friend's attitude made the word of Scripture all the more forceful: 'It is by faith that we understand that the universe was created by God's word, so that what can be seen was made out of what cannot be seen' (Heb 11.3). As believers, we have been gifted with this faith. We can say 'We believe in God, the Father Almighty, maker of heaven and earth and of all things, seen and unseen'. Faith in God and in God's creation provides us with our perspective on the world. Our world is not a closed system, originating through some inexplicable 'big bang'. Our world originates in God's creative love.

Secularist Perspective

The predominant mind set in our society, however, is far removed from the faith vision. It is secularist: that is, the underlying conviction is atheistic, or at least agnostic. The predominant conviction is that the only world that counts is this visible, tangible world, and the only time that matters is the here and now, not some hereafter.

Even when there is no direct denial of a spiritual world there is the prevailing conviction that we can safely ignore those 'spiritual realities' which are grounded in religious faith. Humans do not need a God to be good, or spiritual, or to find complete fulfilment. The inhabitants of this worldview would find it very hard to cope with Pamela. They would, no doubt, respect her, but explain away her deep religious conviction and inner peace as some form of delusion.

The world we live in, and not the faith we profess, can easily form our worldview. Even though we look on ourselves as believers we can look out on the world with the perspective of the unbeliever.

Creation

We cannot think seriously about our world if we ignore the question of creation. Did God create our universe or did it just happen? The answer to that question separates believers from unbelievers. Believers will unhesitatingly affirm belief in creation. Belief in creation, however, does not automatically guarantee a faith perspective on the world. Sometimes we seek to combine personal faith in creation with a perspective on life which basically ignores or denies the implications of such faith. Our life can become compartmentalized. Sunday is for an hour's religion; the rest of the week is 'for business as usual'.

Developing the perspective of faith, however, enables us to discover the loving design of God at the very heart of our history. I discovered this graphically in a man who belonged to that group of prisoners who became known as 'The Birmingham Six'. He was an innocent man and suffered greatly at the time of his arrest. He claimed that a confession was beaten out of him. During a weekend retreat, which I was giving in his prison, he was so cheerful that I asked him how he could keep his spirits up despite all he had suffered. He responded very seriously: 'I can thank God for every day I have been in this prison. Before I was picked up I lived an aimless life. I had no knowledge of God. In this prison I have got to know the Lord in my life and I can live as a free man. When I was outside I imagined I was free. But I wasn't free at all'.

In prison this man had developed a faith perspective on life. Far from inducing a timid, quiescent attitude, his new-found faith fired him with a fearless courage. He challenged each and every injustice in the prison and he fought unflinchingly for the ultimate dismissal of all the charges against him and the others who were wrongly sentenced with him.

The God we worship is not only the God of the sanctuary – of peaceful prayer and liturgy; he is the God of the prison, with his people in their isolation and pain. He is also the God of 'the market place', at the heart of our economic and political life. God is not confined to the churches we build for him.

Years ago I gave a weekend retreat to a group of laymen, basing my reflections on this sentence from the Vatican Council: 'By reason of their special vocation it belongs to the laity to seek the kingdom of God by engaging in temporal affairs and directing them according to God's will'.[1] The message was that they must find God at work, not just in church.

The following year some of that group were back on retreat. One man told me with great joy that he was now finding God everywhere – in his factory, in his social club, and most of all in his garden. He received the grace to to everything 'in the name of Our Lord Jesus Christ'. His whole prayer life was transformed and he lived daily in the presence of God. This gave him a faith perspective on life.

A faith perspective on life is such a blessing when a loved one is dying. I experienced this very vividly when my mother died at the age of 87. For two weeks the whole family gathered to be with her during her last days. Two of us sat with her in her hospital room around the clock. Each evening the rest of us gathered in the home of my brother or sister for Mass and I brought Holy Communion to my mother and those with her. Although she was unable to speak, she was able to receive with great devotion.

Two days before she died she seemed to be in a coma. Her eyes remained tightly closed and her teeth firmly clenched all day. The nurses failed to get her mouth open. I brought Communion that evening as usual, thinking to myself that only my brother and sister would receive. As soon as I entered her room my mother opened her eyes. Her eyes, filled with a most brilliant light, followed me as I crossed the room and left the Blessed Sacrament on the table. I said to my sister 'she has recognized the presence of the Lord'. Then I proceeded with the prayers before Holy Communion.

My mother's eyes were still glowing and fixed on me. I was feeling very elated at the wonderful expression on her face, but sad that she would not be able to open her mouth to receive. The moment I held up the sacred host and said 'Mum, the Body of Christ', her mouth opened wide and she received. Immediately, her eyes closed and her teeth clenched again and she seemed to be back in her coma.

We were privileged to see this moment of transfiguration in her life. The presence of Our Lord in the Blessed Sacrament called her out of a deep coma and filled her with a radiant peace. It was a wonderful confirmation of her faith perspective on life.

In our faith perspective we are aware of God's creative love at the heart of our universe (the mystery of creation); we are aware that we rejected this love and sinned (the mystery of the Fall); we are aware that God did not leave us in our sin but came to rescue us through Christ (the mystery of our redemption); we are aware that Christ suffered and died for us and rose to the new life of the resurrection in order to fill us with the Holy Spirit (the mystery of the Church); we are aware that we are invited to live the life of the Spirit here and now in this life (the mystery of eternal life). Our vision of life in this world is formed and informed by these deep convictions of faith.

Image of God

God reveals to us the mystery of our own being when he declared that we are made in his 'image and likeness' (Gen 1.26). We are not simply 'rational animals', as the ancient Greeks thought; we are separated from the animal kingdom by more than rationality. Nor are we simply some kind of evolutionary phenomenon of nature, as the secularist view would have it. Within that evolutionary process we have been uniquely created by God. God's Spirit teaches us to acknowledge this uniqueness of our creation with this prayer:

> For it was you who created my being,
>   knit me together in my mother's womb.
> I thank you for the wonder of my being,
> for the wonders of your creation.
>
> Ps 139.13

Because we are uniquely created and loved by God we must thank God for the 'wonder of our being', the wonder of ourselves. I will have much more to say about this prayer when we discuss inner healing (see p. 61).

'Seen and Unseen'

We believe that God created an unseen world, an intangible world, which is intimately involved in the drama of our salvation. By very definition the scientist cannot observe or analyse this unseen world. But thousands of believing scientists have found the inspiration for their exploration of the observable world in their faith in the unseen wonders of God's creation.

When I gave a parish mission in Holy Spirit Parish in Huntsville, Alabama, the parish priest boasted that there were more scientists per square foot in his parish than in 'any place else in the world!' Huntsville is the home of Nasa, which has developed the entire American space programme. I was deeply edified and thrilled by the deep faith which I found in so many of those great scientists. At the 5.30 morning Mass throughout the week many of them were there; they were back again for the mission service in the evening.

In this parish I discovered, in flesh and blood, what the Church has always taught, namely that there is no conflict between faith and science. Those scientists making that mission, preached by my confrere Charles Corrigan and myself, were at the forefront of the scientific exploration of space, but each of them personally was deeply engaged in the exploration of his or her own relationship with God. They had a faith perspective on their life and work. Their enthusiasm for journeying into space was fired by their spiritual journey into the mystery of God. The fact that they could not observe or measure the 'unseen world' was no reason for denying its existence. They believed God's Word.

We know of the existence of this spiritual world because

we are told about it in the Bible and the Church professes faith in it.

Angelic World

As well as the physical universe which we can see and observe, we believe in the reality of an angelic world, which we do not see. Many people have had experiences of this angelic world. I consider an experience which I had, while driving my car, an 'angel experience'. I had filled the car with petrol before starting off on a long journey. After driving for thirty minutes, just before I was about to join the motorway, I heard a loud, clear voice which said with a note of alarm 'check the oil'. It was so clear and authoritative that I pulled into the service station which I was about to pass. I checked the oil. The dip stick came up dry! Had I joined the motorway I would have been in big trouble with the engine of the car.

You may have had similar experiences of an invisible, helping and protecting hand in times of danger. Some people would, of course, explain the 'voice' I heard in psychological rather than angelic terms. Since I believe in my guardian angel I find it much more satisfactory to accept that my angel was at hand to help me.

The Church formally professes faith in angels. The Fourth Lateran Council decreed:

There is but one true God . . . the one principle of all things, creator of all things visible and invisible, spiritual and bodily, who, by his almighty power, from the beginning of time has made out of nothing each of these two creatures, spiritual and bodily, that is angelic and belonging to this world.

The First Vatican Council renewed this declaration of faith in the same terms. The new catechism of the Catholic Church, formulating the Church's faith for our time, re-emphasizes the teaching of the Lateran Council and states that 'It is a truth of faith that God created spiritual beings, which we call angels' (para 328). We profess faith not just in the creation of the physical universe that we see around us. We affirm faith in the invisible world that we cannot see. Without revelation from God we cannot know of the reality of this invisible universe. It would be pointless to ask even the greatest scientist whether such a world exists. It is not a question of science, or philosophy, or even of theology. It is a question of faith. The Catholic Church teaches that there is a spiritual world, inhabited by spiritual beings, pure spirits. The Church also believes that some of these pure spirits sinned and became evil spirits, or devils.

Angels

In its liturgy the Church seeks to instil in us a deep awareness that we do not stand alone before God. We are united with the holy angels of God. There is an ancient maxim in theology which states that 'the way the Church prays manifests what the Church believes' (in its Latin form, *'lex orandi, lex credendi'*). If we apply this maxim to the Church's prayers about the holy angels there can be little doubt that the Church firmly believes that these holy angels exist. They exist to help us. As Scripture says 'Are they not all ministering spirits, sent to serve those who are to inherit salvation?' (Heb 1.14).

In the Fourth Eucharistic Prayer we say:

Countless hosts of angels stand before you
    to do your will;
they look upon your splendour
and praise you night and day.
United with them,
and in the name of every creature under
    heaven,
we too praise your glory as we say:
Holy, holy, holy.

In the Preface of every Mass we remind ourselves that we
'join our voices with all the choirs of angels'. In the Mass
we also acknowledge that the angels, like us, praise God
through Christ. We pray in the Preface of the Angels:

Through Christ our Lord
    the great army of angels rejoices in your glory.
In adoration and joy
    we make their hymn of praise our own.

Not only do we renew our faith in the holy angels each
time we celebrate Mass, but the Church also celebrates the
feast of the archangels, Sts Michael, Gabriel and Raphael
(29 September) and the feast of the Guardian Angels (2
October). In the prayers for these feasts we thank God for
the protection of the holy angels:

God our Father, in your loving providence
    you send your holy angels to watch over us.
Hear our prayers,
defend us always with their protection
and let us share your life with them for ever.
                    Prayer from Mass of the Guardian Angels

Since God in his 'loving providence' sends us his angels we, who are always in need of his protection, should surely joyfully accept them. We celebrate the feast of the Guardian Angels because Jesus tells us that God has given to each person a special angel (Mt 18.10).

I am conscious that some fine biblical scholars would not accept what I have just written about angels. The Scriptures, they say, have something very important to say about God and about God's relationship with the world: angels are images or myths or human concepts constructed to convey some truth about God. But angels are not pure spirits. In this view, angels were not created by God; they were created by the poets of the Scriptures as a way of talking about God.

While biblical scholars provide the members of the Church with a great service, it is the Church itself which teaches its members the faith. That is why I have outlined above the official teaching of the Church on the reality of angels. About angels, we believe no more or no less than the Church proposes to our belief. As Cardinal Newman expressed it so beautifully: 'And I hold in veneration, for the love of him alone, holy Church as his creation and her teaching as his own'.

Fallen Angels

The Church clearly teaches the existence of good spirits. But she also believes that, in a most mysterious way, some of these good spirits rebelled against God and lost his grace. They became devils. They used their freedom to sin and rebel against God.

No aspect of Catholic teaching is more offensive to some people than this 'belief in devils'. We do not, of course, 'believe in the devil'. That would be an erroneous way of speaking. Satanists 'believe in the devil'. They put their trust in him. They worship him. We believe that the Word of God tells us about the reality of Satan and his evil spirits. Our faith is in God and in God's revelation.

Pope Paul VI reaffirmed the Church's teaching on the reality of this world of fallen angels: 'Evil is not merely a lack of something, but an effective agent, a living, spiritual being, perverted and perverting. A terrible reality'. And he went on to state that 'It is contrary to the teaching of the Bible and the Church to refuse to recognise the existence of such a reality'.[2] Pope John Paul II, in his encyclical on the Holy Spirit, restates the teaching of the Second Vatican Council and says that Christ 'was crucified and rose again to break the stranglehold of *personified Evil*.[3] There is no doubt about the official teaching of the Catholic Church: the devil and his evil spirits exist. They are hostile to God, enemies of the children of God, implacably opposed to the Kingdom of God.

The reality of evil lies within the experience of each one of us. There are two kinds of evil. The evil of sin, for which we humans are responsible, an evil which manifests itself in exploitation, hatred, murder and violence of all kind. And there is the evil which Pope John Paul II calls 'personified evil', for which we are not responsible, but which constantly seeks to control us through our own sinfulness.

The evil which we see around us cannot simply be reduced to the sum of human wickedness. At the same time, it cannot be explained simply in terms of 'personified evil'. Hence the great need for discernment. As Heinrich Schlier wrote:

Frequently there is only a thin dividing line between good

and bad spirits, and it is only a clear and sharp insight which God grants us that can tell the difference, and dispel the mist which the evil spirit deliberately creates. Where this gift is lacking, there is danger that we may suspect the dark influence of the devil to be at work everywhere, so that we may never recognise him when he is really there; or we may minimise his presence and fail to see him even when he is in our midst.[4]

In a well-known passage C. S. Lewis makes the same point:

There are two equal and opposite errors into which our race can fall about the devils. One is to disbelieve in their existence. The other is to believe, and to feel an excessive and unhealthy interest in them. They themselves are equally pleased by both errors and hail a materialist or a magician with the same delight.[5]

Behind every evil in the world there lurks the reality of the demonic, an invisible, spiritual world, where the powers of darkness are at work. Sin in the human heart, whether it be pride, greed or lust, can open the door to demonic influence. As Pope Paul said: 'This question of the devil and the influence he can exert on individuals as well as communities, whole societies and events, is an important chapter of Catholic doctrine which is given little attention today, though it should be studied again'.[6]

Yet we have to acknowledge that not all Christian theologians and biblical scholars accept the Church's teaching. The view expressed by Francis Wright Beare in his commentary on Matthew's gospel is quite typical:

There is no doubt that the early Christians, like most of

the Jews of the time, believed that there was such a
mighty spirit of evil; nor can we question the fact that
Jesus himself shared these beliefs. None the less, we must
recognise that this is a mythical conception that has lost
appeal to the minds of men; we cannot ourselves accept
it without falling victims to superstition.[7]

This reduction of evil spirits to mythical language has to
be challenged not simply at the biblical and theological
level, but also at the pastoral level. Exorcism is needed
today just as it was needed at the time of Christ. John
Richards has a timely warning for scholars:

> Few theologians appear to have taken any great pains to
> find out what has or has not happened in history, or have
> taken account of anthropology, parapsychology, psychic
> research, comparative religion or spiritualism, before
> assessing what needs to be demythologised. In my own
> limited reading of these subjects, I have encountered
> present-day equivalents of so many New Testament
> phenomena that I would strongly discourage scholars and
> preachers from too great an enthusiasm for dismissing as
> unhistorical what they have not themselves experienced.[8]

Even the pastor or theologian can accept the modern
secularist outlook and assert that since he has never personally experienced people under the influence of evil spirits,
such spirits do not exist. Maybe the reason why he has
never had this experience is because he is convinced that
evil spirits cannot exist!
Biblical theories have pastoral implications. Demythologizing the New Testament teaching on the reality of evil
spirits declares the ministry of exorcism, in all its forms,

obsolete. The discernment of the need for exorcism belongs to pastors and ministers rather than academics and theologians. Academic theories on demythologization have little relevance for those who have been involved in witchcraft and satanist worship or for the victims of such occult practices.

Experience of the Occult Powers

A friend of mine once rang me in a state of great anxiety and fear. She asked me if I could come and celebrate Mass and bless her flat because, she said, 'I am convinced there is some kind of evil presence in my flat and it is due to a prisoner who has taken a hatred to me'. This particular prisoner was serving a life sentence for a murder committed during some kind of satanic ritual. He became a Catholic in prison and Marie was his godmother. He had become very jealous and possessive of her and when she did not give him all her time, but talked to the other men, he vowed to harm her. She described what happened:

He was very upset and angry. He asked me if I would like a 'little visitor' in my flat. Days went by and I began to feel very nervous and anxious about everything. I could not understand what was happening to me. I became afraid of going out, of driving or just meeting people. My flat became very strange and cold at times. I felt there was something or someone there. I began to lose my appetite and lose weight. My sleep was also disturbed. I woke up nearly every night for several weeks in a massive sweat with a feeling of something horrifying in the room.

I continued to go into the prison and I especially hated going in on a Sunday because I knew this prisoner would sit in the front row and leer at me. His face grew more and more awful with horrible sores all over. He told many of the officers and inmates that I was a witch and that he had made a doll of me and was sticking pins in various parts.

One particular night I was so scared that I got the holy water and sprinkled the room and it seemed as if something left and I felt better. I did this every night for a while but I was still feeling scared and as if there was a kind of malign presence in the flat. I started to pray the rosary and kept the rosary in my hand while sleeping, with the holy water near at hand.

A priest friend of mind came and said Mass and blessed the flat. Everything seemed better but there was still something underneath that I could not put my finger on. This priest said I should also pray for the prisoner, which I found difficult to do after all the suffering he caused me. At any rate I did pray for him and almost immediately all the fear, anxiety and terror left me and I became my old self again.

When I returned to the prison on the next Sunday the prisoner was still sitting on the front row – but this time he had his head down. After Mass he approached me and fell on his knees before me, begging for pardon. He said that something had happened to him during the week. All anger and hatred had left him. He admitted that he wanted to cause me harm – actual death if possible.

The occult powers which that prisoner was trying to use against Marie were defeated by the symbols of faith, namely holy water and the rosary, and by the Mass and her prayers for his salvation. She was not set free by reducing everything to an over-active imagination. She wrote: 'I told the chaplain about my concerns and about how I was feeling and my problems in the flat and how I was having problems sleeping. I was told that if I took a good glass of whisky before I went to bed I would be fine. Needless to say it didn't work'.

Some years ago my confrere Fr Ahearn and I were asked by a religious Sister to help four sixth form girls. They had been experimenting with the ouija board. When we arrived at the convent we found these young ladies in the grip of fear: they could not sleep, eat, or concentrate on their work. They had been contaminated by some kind of evil beyond their understanding. They knew, in their own experience, the cruel reality of the demonic. They also experienced the power of Jesus setting them free when I uttered a silent prayer.

For years I discussed the ministry of exorcism with an eminent theologian who is now deceased. He was firmly convinced that the devil does not exist. His pastoral view of things was this: no devil, no evil spirits, no ministry of exorcism or deliverance. Yet he always loved to hear stories of deliverance. He was fascinated by how those four girls were set free from contamination with the ouija board by a silent prayer of command in the name of Jesus. I would put this question to him: Explain how a silent prayer of command in the name of Jesus can set people free from such contamination and from burdens which they have carried for years and from which no therapy could release them? He always refused to answer. Since the prayer was in silence he could not explain the fruit of the prayer in psychological terms. It could not be autosuggestion! He would always smile when I would say 'don't you see that the real explanation is that something heard and something obeyed?'

The evil spirit heard the silent command in the name of Jesus and departed.

Pastoral theology and practice must be based not on biblical or theological theories but on pastoral experience. Good theology is never just a reflection on the reflections of others; good theology is always a reflection on the experience of the People of God. The experience is that people are not freed from molestation by evil spirits through biblical theories, which deny their existence, but through ministry in the name of Jesus, which casts them out. We will consider this in more detail later on (see p. 104f).

Catholic Worldview

The Catholic worldview includes, then, not just the visible world, which we can see, but the angelic world, which we cannot see. At the heart of the Catholic worldview, the Catholic *weltanschauung*, there is an orientation to the supernatural, the spiritual, the unseen, the intangible. Our vision is informed by our faith in Christ, seated at the right hand of God in glory.

Pamela had that vision. Because of her experience of Christ she could say, despite all her suffering, 'I wouldn't have missed it for anything'. The prisoner who was unjustly sentenced has that faith vision. He could say 'I can thank God for every day I have spent in this prison'. Marie has that vision. When she was attacked by evil powers she used active prayer and her faith in the power of God, symbolized in holy water and the rosary, to resist.

Each of us should be seeking daily to form this faith vision for ourselves. Within this worldview it is logical for the Church to honour the holy angels and, at the same time, to warn us to be on our guard against the wiles of the devil. In the Lord's Prayer, Jesus himself taught us to pray to the Father to be 'delivered from the evil one'.

Since the Church believes strongly in the reality of this spiritual world, where the holy angels exist to worship God and serve humankind, and also where the devil and his evil spirits exist to oppose God and destroy humankind, the Vatican Council had no hesitation in declaring that 'A monumental struggle against the powers of darkness pervades the whole of human history. The battle was joined from the origins of the world and will continue until the last day, as the Lord attests'.[9]

Since earliest times, the Church has urged her members to be aware of this spiritual struggle at the heart of history and to use the spiritual weapons of prayer, fasting and intercession to defend themselves against all attacks of the devil. The Church too has never hesitated to use the ministry of exorcism to expel evil spirits from people whom they have possessed.

At the same time, the Church has never exaggerated the reality of the demonic. The devil is a creature. He is a fallen angel. As such, the devil is limited in both his knowledge and power. The Church has always assured her members that those who live in the light of God, those who pray to the Father and turn to Christ for the forgiveness of their sins, have no need to fear 'the powers of darkness'. When we walk in the light, the darkness cannot touch us. That is why, although we believe that the devil exists, we live our lives, under the Lordship of Jesus, undisturbed by his existence. In fact, as Dom Benedict Heron has rightly observed, 'Satan and the demons have more to fear from us than we have from them, if we keep our eyes fixed on Jesus and if his praises are on our lips and in our hearts'.[10]

2

Christ and the Spiritual World

The promise of God to humankind is summed up in the words of the prophet Joel: 'After this I will pour out my spirit on all mankind' (Joel 3.1). God, who is spirit, wants to dwell with us, who are flesh.

God promises us his Spirit to overcome the devastation and alienation caused by sin. When God created us he declared that we were 'very good' (Gen 1.3.). God loved us. Yet, despite God's great love for us we sinned. We cut ourselves off from God. Through our sin we entered into a state of alienation: alienation from God, from neighbour, from ourselves.

In our sinful state of alienation we had lost our way and lost our capacity for life with God. God, however, had compassion on us. Because he loved us 'with an everlasting love', his love could not change. Despite our sin and alienation we remained 'precious in his sight' (Is 43.10). God determined to redeem us. We would have to be created afresh, born again. God planned a new creation in which we would be reborn of the Holy Spirit. God announced this new creation, this new birth in the Holy Spirit, through the prophets.

In the prophecy of Jeremiah God promised to enter into

a new covenant with his people: 'This is the covenant I will make with the House of Israel when those days arrive – it is Yahweh who speaks. Deep within them I will plant my law, writing it on their hearts. Then I will be their God and they will be my people' (31.31). In the prophecy of Ezekiel God promised a new heart: 'I will give you a new heart and put a new spirit in you; I shall remove the heart of stone from your bodies and give you a heart of flesh instead. I shall put my spirit in you . . .' (Ezek 36.26). In the prophecy of Joel, God summed up all his promises in these words: 'After this I will pour out my spirit upon all mankind' (Joel 3:1).

God's intention, then, is clear. He wants to overcome the alienation caused by sin. He wants to unite himself to us, in his Spirit, so that we may live through his Spirit. God fulfilled all these promises through Our Lord Jesus Christ. St Paul writes: 'however many the promises God made, the Yes to them all is in him' (2 Cor 2.20). It was not only through Jesus, but also in Jesus that God fulfilled his promises.

Jesus: Man of the Spirit

Through his Incarnation the Son of God became one of us. He took on our human nature, with all its weakness. Jesus' first claim about himself was that God had fulfilled his promise and poured out his Spirit. He read the passage: 'The spirit of the Lord has been given to me, for he has anointed me' (Lk 4.18) and he told his hearers: 'This text of scripture is being fulfilled today even as you listen' (Lk 4.22).

Jesus presents himself to the people as the one on whom the Father has poured out the Spirit. Jesus is flesh, like us.

The Father's promise was to 'pour out the Spirit on all flesh'. Jesus is now claiming that the Father has fulfilled that promise. At the very conception of Jesus the Holy Spirit was active. The angel announced to Mary 'The Holy Spirit will come upon you and the power of the Most High will cover you with its shadow' (Lk 1.35).

Jesus was conceived through the power of the Holy Spirit. God the Son entered our history; he became a human being like us; he was born, through the power of the Holy Spirit, of Mary his virgin mother. He was endowed with all our human faculties: a human mind and heart, human emotions and intelligence, human hopes and desires. Jesus, by divine nature the Son of God, by human nature the Son of Mary, is forever totally identified with our sinful human history and destiny.

At the very conception of Jesus, then, there was an outpouring of the Holy Spirit. God's promise to 'pour out the Spirit' was being fulfilled.

This mystery of the Incarnation is at the very centre of our Christian faith. We believe not just that Jesus was the greatest prophet and spiritual leader of all times. We believe that while being fully human, sharing in all our human weakness, Jesus was the Son of the living God. Although Jesus became like us in all things but sin, there can never be another human being like him in his unique oneness with God.

Once when I was giving a retreat to a community of religious men an elderly brother asked to see me. He said to me, 'You are talking a great deal about the Father of Jesus. That was St Joseph, wasn't it?' This was a totally unexpected comment. I tried rather clumsily to explain that St Joseph was the foster father of Jesus. Jesus was conceived by the Holy Spirit. God was his Father. And so, I said, we

believe that Jesus is God, equal to the Father. He looked
at me for some time, absorbing what I was trying to say.
Then he replied 'Well, I still think the Father is a superior
being'.

The fact that this man lived his life in a religious community and, through no apparent fault of his own, did not
accurately profess the faith of the Church in the divinity of
Jesus Christ puzzled me. He was probably never asked in
his whole life: 'Do you believe that Jesus is the Son of God
equal to the Father'? It would have been presumed that as
a practising Catholic, wanting to dedicate his life to God,
he would believe in the Incarnation. Could it be that there
are others who while professing faith do not really believe
in the total reality of the mystery of the Incarnation? That in
every way Jesus is human, and in every way he is divine? I
was forced to examine my own faith.

We are not expected to understand how Jesus, whom we
can see as a baby in his mother's arms, could at the same
time be God. Even more challenging, we cannot see how
Jesus, dying on the cross, could at the same time be the
living God. If we could see his divinity there would be no
need for faith. Indeed, Jesus himself tells us that 'no one
has seen God'. We cannot see God with our human eyes.
We cannot, therefore, see God in Jesus with our human
eyes. His divinity, hidden in his humanity, is disclosed only
to the eye of faith.

Faith in Christ's divinity is at the heart of all Christian
faith. 'The divinity of Christ is the cornerstone holding up
the two mysteries of the Trinity and the Incarnation. Take
this stone away and the whole structure of Christian faith
collapses'.[1] We believe that God, the creator of the universe,
is so present in our human history that Jesus of Nazareth,
born of the virgin Mary, is at the same time the eternal

Son of God. The world into which Jesus was born was created through him and for him. As Scripture says: 'He is the image of the unseen God and is the first born of all creation, for in him were created all things in heaven and on earth: everything visible and everything invisible, Thrones, Dominations, Sovereignties, Powers – all things were created through him and for him' (Col 1.15–16). Everything that is, including ourselves, was created in and through and for Christ. Sin usurped the very purpose of our creation. Sin denied that we belonged to Christ. That is why Christ himself came to save us.

The Promise Fulfilled: Jesus Baptized in the Holy Spirit

St Luke describes the scene well: 'Now when all the people had been baptised and while Jesus after his own baptism was at prayer, heaven opened and the Holy Spirit descended on him in bodily shape, like a dove. And a voice came from heaven, "You are my Son, the Beloved; my favour rests on you" ' (Lk 3.21). God the Father had promised to pour out his Spirit. He has now fulfilled his promise. He has poured out the Spirit on Jesus.

Jesus was not baptized with the Spirit through the baptism of John the Baptist. Jesus was at prayer when the Father baptized him in the Holy Spirit. John is the witness. He tells us: 'I saw the Spirit coming down on him from heaven like a dove and resting on him. I did not know him myself, but he who sent me to baptise with water had said to me, "the man on whom you see the Spirit come down and rest is the one who is going to baptise with the Holy Spirit" ' (Jn 1.31). While Jesus was at prayer John saw the

Spirit descend. The outpouring of the Spirit was the
Father's response to the prayer of Jesus.

It is surely fitting that on the occasion of the fulfilment
of God's promise to pour out his Spirit we should get a
glimpse of the mystery not only of the person of Jesus but
also of the God of the promise. The voice acknowledges
Jesus with the words 'You are my Son, the Beloved'; it not
only confirms the testimony of John the Baptist but also
reveals another more profound dimension of the truth
about Jesus of Nazareth as Messiah. It is this: *the Messiah
is the beloved Son of the Father*. This solemn exaltation cannot
be reduced to the messianic mission of the Servant of the
Lord.[2]

The 'voice' says to Jesus not only that he is 'Son', but
also that he is 'the Beloved'. Jesus is being told by the
Father what kind of Messiah he is going to be. He would
not be the political, triumphant Messiah whom the people
were expecting, the Messiah who would liberate them from
the oppression of the Romans. He would be the suffering
servant of the Lord, the Messiah in whom the servant
prophecies of Isaiah would be fulfilled: 'Here is my servant whom I uphold, my chosen one in whom my soul
delights. I have endowed him with my spirit, that he may
bring true justice to the nations' (Is 42.1).

Jesus knew the prophecies. He knew that he was chosen
to be the 'suffering servant', the 'man of sorrows and familiar with suffering' (Is 53.3). He will be able to say to the
two disciples on the road to Emmaus, after his Resurrection, ' "You foolish men! So slow to believe the full message
of the prophets. Was it not ordained that the Christ should
suffer and so enter into his glory?" Then, starting with
Moses and going through the prophets, he explained to

them the passages throughout the scriptures that were
about himself' (Lk 24.25–7).

When the Father pours out the Holy Spirit he declares
that Jesus is at one and the same time the eternal Son and
the promised Messiah. 'Messiah' means 'the anointed one'.
Jesus was anointed with the Holy Spirit. As St Peter said,
'God anointed him with the Holy Spirit and with power,
and because God was with him, Jesus went about doing
good and curing all who had fallen into the power of the
devil' (Acts 10.38).

Jesus: Led by the Spirit

Jesus' immediate response to this gift of the Father is to
allow the Spirit to guide him. St Luke says 'he was led by
the Spirit'. This is a new experience of the Spirit for Jesus.
The experience of being 'filled with the Spirit' was the gift
of the Father; the experience of being 'led by the Spirit'
was Jesus' response to the gift. Having received the gift of
the Spirit from the Father, Jesus had to decide not just
what to do next; rather, he had to decide what he would
allow the Spirit to do. And he allowed the Spirit to lead
him.

The Spirit would lead Jesus only into doing the will of
the Father. In preparation for doing the Father's will, in the
work of our salvation, the Spirit led Jesus into the wilderness
where he fasted and prayed for forty days and where he
encountered the evil spirit, Satan. It is surely significant
that when the Holy Spirit had been poured out the evil
spirit manifests himself. The evil spirit had to investigate
who Jesus was. He had his suspicions, but he was not sure:
'If you are the Son of God tell these stones to turn into
loaves' (Mt 4.2).

Commenting on the temptations of Jesus, L. Howard Marshall writes: 'Jesus certainly took for granted the reality of Satan'.[3] Montague in his commentary on the temptations as recorded in Mark's Gospel writes:

> Mark is not concerned, as are Matthew and Luke, with the specific temptations but with the fact that the entire period is one of conflict, and the adversary is Satan. By introducing this protagonist, Mark informs us from the very beginning that Jesus' ministry will be a wrestling not with flesh and blood but with principalities and powers (cf. Eph 6.12). Jesus' conflict with Satan does not end in the desert; it only begins there. In his public ministry he will confront Satan in those possessed (1.23; 5.2; 7.25; 9.17 etc.), in the testing questions of his opponents (8.11; 10.2; 12.15) and even in the blind resistance of his own disciples (8.33). Satan is the strong man, but Jesus has come as the stronger one to bind him (1.7; 3.27). If we would understand Jesus as Mark understands him, we must accept this role of the demonic antagonism throughout the gospel.[4]

In his own experience of temptation, Jesus knew the reality of the demonic; in his experience of exorcism he saw the victory of God's Kingdom over the power of evil; in his death and Resurrection he would know the full victory over evil. As St John said: 'It was to undo all that the devil had done that the Son of God appeared' (1 Jn 3.8).

Jesus: In the Power of the Spirit

Jesus is prepared to face this demonic antagonism because, as St Luke says, he returned from the Jordan 'with the power of the Spirit in him'. Jesus begins his ministry of proclaiming the Gospel in the power of the Spirit.

In becoming man Jesus entered into our human weakness. In that state of weakness he was always in union with his Father, always doing what pleased the Father, but he was not ready for his ministry. He had to wait until he was empowered by the Spirit. The Gospel, as St Luke reminds us, consists of 'everything which Jesus did and taught' (Acts 1.1). The Gospel consists of both the works and the words of Jesus. For a long time I tended to separate the works of Jesus from the words of Jesus. I would then present the Gospel entirely in terms of the words. In this way, while remaining very faithful to the words, I really overlooked his works. In a sense I 'verbalised' the Gospel.

Jesus exercised a fourfold ministry of preaching and teaching, of healing the sick and exorcising evil spirits. If we separate what Jesus did from what he taught we can easily reduce his ministry to preaching and teaching and ignore his ministry of healing and exorcism. We might even be saying to ourselves, as I think I was, that whereas his teaching and preaching are relevant for every age, his healings and exorcisms were peculiar to Jesus himself and relevant for his own age and culture alone.

Yet Jesus himself promised that his disciples would continue to do the same works that he himself did. He performed all his works through the power of the Holy Spirit. Since he was giving the same Spirit to his disciples he expected them to do the same works. We have to see the relationship between Jesus' ministry and the power of the Spirit. Our very faith in his divine sonship may incline us to ascribe what Jesus did to his divinity. For many years I think that was what I was doing.

In fact, I used the miracles of Jesus to prove that he was

divine. Since, in my perception, the miracles proved that he
was divine, I was never able to take this promise seriously: 'I
tell you most solemnly, whoever believes in me will perform
the same works as I do myself, he will perform even greater
works, because I am going to the Father' (Jn 14.12). How
could I do the same works that Jesus did? It was like a new
revelation to me when I saw, for the first time, that the
Holy Spirit was the source of Christ's ministry. I was so
accustomed to thinking that Jesus worked through his own
divine power that I had not noticed that it was through the
power of the Spirit that Jesus was exercising his ministry. I
was in danger of missing an essential aspect of the Incarnation: 'He emptied himself, to assume the condition of a
slave, and became as men are' (Phil 2.7). My friend on
retreat, whom I mentioned above, found it hard to accept
that Jesus was really divine; I was in danger of unconsciously not believing that he was really human, sharing
fully in our weak human nature.

Jesus specifically identifies the Holy Spirit as the source
of his power of exorcism. The Pharisees accused him of
exorcising evil spirits through the power of Beezlebub. In
defence of his ministry Jesus says: 'But if it is through the
Spirit of God that I cast devils out, then know that
the kingdom of God has overtaken you' (Mt 12.28).

The sign of the presence of the Kingdom, which Jesus is
proclaiming, is what the Holy Spirit is doing through him.
James Dunn comments:

The eschatological kingdom was present for Jesus
because the eschatological Spirit was present in and
through him. In other words, it was not so much a case
of 'Where I am there is the kingdom', as 'Where the

Spirit is there is the kingdom'. It was the manifestation of the power of God which was the sign of the kingdom.[5]

St Luke recounts the controversy over exorcism in the context of the Lord's teaching on prayer. Jesus has taught the disciples the Lord's prayer and has encouraged them to ask the Father for what they need. 'So I say to you ask and it will be given to you; search and you will find; knock and the door will be opened to you'. He concludes this great exhortation on asking with the words: 'If you then, who are evil, know how to give your children what is good, how much more will the heavenly Father give the Holy Spirit to those who ask him' (Lk 11.12). In the very next sentence Luke says: 'He was casting out a devil and it was dumb'. John P. Kealy writes 'Consideration of the gift of the Holy Spirit (God's kingdom in action) leads Luke to consider the opposing spirits and the temptation of Jesus to perform a sign'.[6]

Jesus, empowered by the Spirit, proclaims the Kingdom of God. To the poor, he preaches good news from God; when he encounters evil spirits, he casts them out; sick people who come to him are healed. He sent his disciples forth to do as he was doing:

After this the Lord appointed seventy-two others and sent them out ahead of him, in pairs, to all the towns and places he himself was to visit. He said to them . . . 'Whenever you go into a town where they make you welcome, eat what is set before you. Cure those in it who are sick and say, "The kingdom of God is very near you" ' (Lk 10.1/8).

When the disciples returned from this mission and were

recounting to Jesus all that they had accomplished in his name ('even the devils submit to us when we use your name'), Jesus had a wonderful experience of the Spirit:

> It was then that, filled with joy by the Holy Spirit, he said. 'I bless you, Father of heaven and earth, for hiding these things from the learned and the clever and revealing them to mere children. . . . Everything has been given to me by my Father; and no one knows who the Son is except the Father, and who the Father is except the Son and those to whom the Son chooses to reveal him' (Lk 10.21–2).

Jesus rejoices in the Spirit because he can reveal the Father to 'mere children', to his disciples. Pope John Paul II writes:

> The union of Christ with the Holy Spirit, a union of which he is perfectly aware, is expressed in that 'rejoicing', which in a certain way renders 'perceptible' its hidden source. Thus there is a particular manifestation and rejoicing which is proper to the Son of Man, the Christ-Messiah, whose humanity belongs to the person of the Son of God, substantially one with the Holy Spirit in divinity.[7]

In his whole being Christ was filled with the Holy Spirit; in all his ministry he was empowered by the Spirit; in his labours for the Kingdom of God he rejoiced in the Spirit.

The Spirit of God, who was so active in Christ throughout his public ministry of preaching the Gospel, was not absent from his great work through which he redeemed us, namely, his death on the cross. Scripture tells us that 'Christ offered himself as the perfect sacrifice to God through the eternal Spirit' (Heb 9.14).

Christ's death was life-giving for us, because Christ died through the power of the Holy Spirit. Through that same Holy Spirit, who is 'the Lord, the giver of life', Christ was raised into the new life of the Resurrection. Filled with the new life of the Resurrection, by the power of the Holy Spirit, Jesus came to his disciples in the upper room on Easter Sunday evening and greeted them with the words 'Peace be with you'. Then, he said to them, 'As the Father sent me, so am I sending you'. After saying this he breathed on them and said: 'Receive the Holy Spirit. For whose sins you forgive they are forgiven; for whose sins you retain, they are retained' (Jn 20.22–3).

Jesus gives to his disciples the very same gift which he himself had received from the Father. He says 'receive the gift of the Holy Spirit'. He empowers them with the same power with which he had been empowered by the Father, the power of the Spirit. He entrusts to them the same mission which he himself had received from the Father, the mission of preaching the Gospel. What Jesus did through the power of the Spirit, while he walked this earth, he will continue to do through his disciples because his disciples will have his Spirit.

In the Fourth Eucharistic Prayer the Church sums up everything I have been trying to say in this chapter:

And that we might live no longer for ourselves but for him, he sent the Holy Spirit from you, Father, as his first gift to those who believe, *to complete his work on earth* and bring us the fullness of grace.

In Jesus we see all the promises of God our Father fulfilled:

the Spirit is poured out; the new covenant is established; our sins are forgiven; we are reconciled with our Father; the Gospel of reconciliation is preached to the ends of the earth. All these promises are fulfilled because Jesus, the man filled with the Spirit, says to his disciples in every age: 'Receive the Holy Spirit'! Live through my Spirit; be empowered by my Spirit; work through my Spirit. The wonder of our salvation is that Jesus shares fully with us that Holy Spirit whom he received from God his Father. As St John exclaimed, 'Indeed, from his fullness we have all received – yes, grace in return for grace' (Jn 1.16).

3

Jesus: Our Intercessor at the Right Hand of the Father

In one of the penitential rites of the Mass we say to Christ: 'You are pleading for us now at the right hand of the Father, Lord have mercy on us'. This prayer of the Mass focuses on Christ's role as our intercessor. As Scripture says, 'his power to save is utterly certain, since he is living to intercede for all who come to God through him' (Heb 8.25).

We put our faith and trust in the risen Christ, now seated at the right hand of the Father in glory, interceding for us.

Jesus' Prayer for Another Advocate

The whole object of Christ's intercession with the Father is the outpouring of the Spirit. He promised his disciples: 'I shall ask the Father, and he will give you another Advocate to be with you for ever, that Spirit of truth whom the world can never receive since it neither sees nor knows him; but you know him because he is with you, he is in you' (Jn 14. 16–18). In response to this intercession of Jesus, the Father sent the other Advocate. He poured out his Spirit on the disciples. This is the mystery of Pentecost, the mystery of the Church.

The Second Vatican Council has made it very clear that

the Church is established by Christ when the Spirit is poured out: 'By communicating his Spirit to his brothers, called together from all people, Christ made them mystically his own body'.[1]

> Rising from the dead, He sent his life-giving Spirit upon his disciples and through this Spirit has established his body, the Church, as the universal sacrament of salvation.[2]
>
> After being lifted up on the cross and glorified, the Lord Jesus poured forth the Spirit whom he had promised, and through whom he called and gathered the people of the New Covenant.[3]

The Council teaches that the Church is the direct result of Christ's action of sending his Spirit. For a long time, I think, my view of the origin of the Church took this form: Jesus established his Church while he was on earth; he then sent his Spirit to sanctify and guide the Church.

I believed that the Spirit was in the Church. I did not, however, realize that it was the Spirit himself who created the Church. I think this was because I had failed to grasp the ongoing relationship between Jesus and the Spirit. I did not see the outpouring of the Spirit on Jesus as the fulfilment of the Father's promise. As a consequence I did not focus on Jesus as the man of the Spirit, the man filled with the Spirit and empowered for his ministry by the Spirit. My focus was on the divinity of Christ.

Jesus shares with us what he received from his Father. Jesus was anointed with the fullness of the Spirit by the Father. He shares that Spirit with us. Indeed, someone has aptly defined the Church in this way: 'the community of those who share in the anointing of the Anointed One'.

Jesus cannot share with us the unique union with God
whereby he and the Father are one. We call that union the
'hypostatic union' – unique to Jesus and incommunicable
to us. He can communicate to us what he received from
the Father, namely the Holy Spirit. This communication
of the Spirit, this imparting of the Spirit, is the creation of
the Church.

The Church comes into being through Christ's intercession: 'I will ask the Father and he will give you another
Paraclete' (Jn 14.16). St John describes in detail how this
gift of the other Paraclete was given:

> In the evening of that same day, the first day of the week,
> the doors were closed in the room where the disciples
> were, for fear of the Jews. Jesus came and stood among
> them. He said to them, 'Peace be with you,' and
> showed them his hands and his side. The disciples were
> filled with joy when they saw the Lord, and he said to
> them again, 'Peace be with you. As the Father sent me,
> so am I sending you.' After saying this he breathed on
> them and said: 'Receive the Holy Spirit' (Jn 20. 19–22).

Reflecting on this passage Pope John Paul writes:

> The Risen Christ, as it were beginning a new creation,
> 'brings' to the Apostles the Holy Spirit. He brings him
> at the price of his own 'departure': he gives them this
> Spirit as it were through the wounds of his crucifixion:
> 'He showed them his hands and his side'. It is in the
> power of this crucifixion that he says to them: 'Receive
> the Holy Spirit.'[4]

Jesus, the suffering Servant of the Lord, pleads for us

through his Passion and death. As the prophet foretold: 'By
his sufferings shall my servant justify many, taking their
faults on himself . . . and praying all the time for sinners'
(Is 53.12). Through this powerful intercession, Christ won
for us our salvation, the gift of the Holy Spirit.

With the coming of the Spirit the era of the Church
began. As Pope John Paul said, 'The time of the Church
began at the moment when the promises and predictions
that so explicitly refer to the Counsellor, the Spirit of truth,
began to be fulfilled in complete power and clarity upon
the Apostles, thus determining the birth of the Church'.[5]

St Matthew gives us a different insight into the mystery
of the Church. Jesus says to his disciples: 'Go, therefore,
make disciples of all nations; baptise them in the name of
the Father and the Son and the Holy Spirit, and teach them
to observe all the commands I gave you. And know that I
am with you always; yes, to the end of time' (Mt 28: 19–20).
St Matthew does not record the fact that Jesus either asks
the Father for the Spirit or imparts it to the disciples.
George Montague explains why:

> The reason appears to be that Matthew considers the
> resurrection and glorification of Jesus to be his entering,
> not heaven, but the church as an abiding presence. He
> is the promised Immanuel (1.23) whose final words to
> the church are: 'I am with you all days, even to the
> consummation of the world' (28.20). That means,
> though, that the Spirit which the Father places upon
> Jesus (3.11; 12.28) rests upon the church which is one
> with him. The church has the Spirit, then, not because
> Jesus left the Spirit as his replacement until he returns
> (the view of Luke and John) or because at some moment
> during his ministry or after the resurrection he specifi-

cally conveyed the Spirit to the church, but rather because, remaining with the church, Jesus baptises with the Spirit through sharing his own baptism with the disciples of all ages. Jesus does not give the Spirit to the church but rather receives it for the church. Whence the intimate and necessary identification of Christian baptism with his.[6]

The Spirit is given in response to Jesus' prayer: Jesus prayed at the Jordan and the Spirit was given to himself; he asked the Father again and the Spirit was given to us. Jesus knows the power of intercession.

Jesus also knows the power of the Spirit. He told his disciples: 'You will receive power when the Spirit comes and then you will be my witnesses, not only in Jerusalem but throughout Judaea and Samaria, and indeed to the ends of the earth' (Acts 1.8). He knew the power of the Spirit in his own life. He wants his disciples to know that same power. Indeed, in their joy and enthusiasm after the Resurrection he had to warn them not to begin their proclamation of the Gospel without that power: 'Stay in the city then, until you are clothed with the power from on high' (Luke 24.49).

Jesus is interceding not just for the Spirit of truth, who will guide his disciples throughout the ages, but for the Spirit of empowerment. He knows our weakness: he experienced the fragility of his own first disciples. They all deserted him. Yet Jesus had such confidence in the transforming presence of the Holy Spirit that he assured his weak and facilitating followers that they would be empowered for their mission, and that they would bring the Gospel to the ends of the earth.

Jesus' confidence in the Spirit was not disappointed. No

sooner had the Spirit come upon them than the disciples
began preaching the Gospel. On Pentecost day itself the
preaching of Peter converted three thousand men and
women! Jesus promised his disciples: 'I tell you solemnly,
whoever believes in me will perform the same works as I
do myself, he will perform even greater works, because I am
going to the Father' (Jn 14.12). We see this promise fulfilled
in the ministry of Peter who immediately began doing the
works Jesus did: preaching the Gospel; healing the sick;
casting out evil spirits; even raising the dead to life. St Luke
describes the enthusiasm and the miracles in Jerusalem in
this way:

> So many signs and wonders were worked among the
> people at the hands of the apostles that the sick were
> even taken out into the streets and laid on beds and
> sleeping-mats in the hope that at least the shadow of
> Peter might fall across some of them as he went past.
> People even came crowding in from the towns around
> about Jerusalem, bringing with them their sick and those
> tormented by unclean spirits, and all of them were cured'
> (Acts 5.12–16).

Stephen, the first martyr, 'was filled with grace and power
and began to work miracles and great signs among the
people' (Acts 6.8), while St Paul tells us how he brought
the Gospel to the Thessalonians: 'We know, brothers, that
God loves you and that you have been chosen, because
when we brought the Good News to you, it came to you
not only in words, but as power and as the Holy Spirit
and as utter conviction' (1 Thess 1.4). And writing to the
Romans Paul is able to say: 'I think I have some reason to
be proud of what I, in union with Christ Jesus, have been

able to do for God. What I am presuming to speak of, of
course, is only what Christ himself has done to win the
allegiance of the pagans, using what I have said and done,
by the power of signs and wonders, by the power of the
Holy Spirit' (Rom 15.17–19).

Wherever we follow the footsteps of the apostles and the
early disciples of Christ we find the Lord's promise fulfilled.
They are doing the same work that he did. They are doing
even greater works because now Jesus is at the right hand
of the Father and is present in all his power with them.

Jesus had promised that he would ask the Father for the
Spirit. He promised that the disciples would receive power
when the Spirit came. And they did! Power to preach;
power to heal; power to cast out evil spirits. We have to see
that whole exciting beginning of the Church, as described
by St Luke in Acts, as the answer to Christ's intercession.
Or we can see the disciples' powerful ministry through the
eyes of St Mark: 'And so the Lord Jesus, after he had
spoken to them, was taken up into heaven: there at the
right hand of God he took his place, while they, going out,
preached everywhere, the Lord working with them and
confirming the word by the signs that accompanied it' (Mk
16.19–20).

'The Lord working with them': that is the essence of
Christian ministry. St Matthew has the same emphasis as
St Mark: 'know I am with you always, yes, to the end of
time' (Mt. 28.20). The disciple is never alone. The Lord
is working with him or her in every situation. And just as
the Lord himself worked through the power of the Holy
Spirit so he is enabling his disciples today to work through
that same power.

The manifestation of the power of the Spirit, through
works of healing and deliverance from evil spirits, did not

cease with the death of the last apostle. We find the same striking manifestation of the power of the Spirit in the early centuries of the history of the Church. Before we look at some of the witnesses from these early centuries, let us digress a little and reflect on the sanctifying role of the Spirit.

The Sanctifying Role of Spirit

The primary role of the Holy Spirit is the sanctification of God's people. The Spirit dwells in the heart of each one of us. This abiding presence of the Spirit is given for our rebirth as God's children. As St Paul said, 'the proof that you are sons is that God sent the Spirit of his Son into our hearts; the Spirit that cries, "Abba", "Father" ' (Gal 4.7). By sending us the Spirit, Jesus not only created the Church but, through the Spirit in our hearts, God established his new covenant with us.

That word 'covenant' is not an easy word to understand or explain. For years I tried to preach about it. I would try to explain that a covenant was like a pact, or an agreement, made, not between equals but between two unequals. For example, a king could enter into an agreement with one of his subjects. Being king he did not have to enter any agreement. But once he entered into an agreement, that agreement would be a covenant between him and his subject and he would have to honour it. The marvel of a covenant between God and us is that God honours his covenant: he is, as it were, bound by it.

I had a very objective or intellectual understanding of covenant. Then one day in 1968, when I was teaching moral theology in our seminary, I came across the teaching of St Thomas Aquinas. St Thomas was not talking about pacts or agreements. He wrote: 'The New Covenant consists in the inpouring of the Holy Spirit'[7] and in another commentary he said: 'As the Holy Spirit works in us charity which is the fullness of the Law, he himself is the New Covenant'.[8]

For days I pondered those texts. How did we lose sight of them? If St Thomas, who is recognized as the greatest theologian in the history of the Church, was teaching in the thirteenth century that 'the Holy Spirit is the New Covenant' why did we not receive that teaching in our catechism? I began to say to myself, 'the covenant is not just some kind of objective pact or agreement; the covenant is a person, the divine person of the Holy Spirit!'

We call ourselves 'the people of the New Covenant'. But should we not personalize covenant, as St Thomas did, and call ourselves 'the people of the Holy Spirit'? The Vatican Council speaks of 'the priests of the New Covenant': should priests not personalize this for themselves and see themselves as Christ's priests of the Holy Spirit? And if we are priests of the Holy Spirit should we not live and work through the Spirit?

Whatever your vocation in the Church, married or single, religious, laity or priest, you are a person of the New Covenant. You are a person of the Holy Spirit. Therefore, you live and work in and through the Spirit. We receive this sanctifying gift of the Spirit as a totally unmerited grace of God. Jesus intercedes for us and the Father gives us the Spirit. God wants to form us in the 'perfect image of his Son' (Rom 8.29). He wants to reproduce in us that same life in the Spirit which Jesus had, because he loves us 'just as he loved Jesus'. As people of the New Covenant, people of the Holy Spirit, God wants our life in the Spirit to be patterned on Christ's life in the Spirit. It took me a very long time before I could really accept with my heart this amazing good news that what God did in Jesus, through the Spirit, he wants to do in us through the same Spirit.

St Luke highlights the pattern of Christ's relationship with the Spirit in this way.

Jesus was filled with the Spirit   That was God the Father's gift to him. He gives that same gift to us.

Jesus was led by the Spirit   That was Jesus' response to the gift of God's Spirit. He surrendered, so that he could be led. If we wish to be led by the Spirit we must surrender just as Jesus did. His prayer of surrender 'not my will, but thine be done' must become our prayer.

Jesus was empowered by the Spirit   In his human weakness the power of the Spirit is present so that he can do the works his Father gives him to do. We too in our weakness must do God's work. We receive the same empowerment of the Holy Spirit.

There is a great difference between 'doing God's work' and 'working for God'. The empowerment of the Spirit is for doing God's work. Therefore at the heart of our ministry there must always be a prayerful and listening reference to God: does God want me to do this? Is this good work, which I am proposing to do, God's will, or is it just my holy will? There is no empowerment of the Spirit for us to do our holy will!

Sometimes, I feel, we tackle good works, plan great apostolic projects, without enquiring whether God wants us to do such a work at all. Then we storm heaven for God's blessing on a project which God may never have wanted in the first place! If we are working 'in union with the Holy

Spirit' we must surely always ask him, before we begin any work, whether our proposed project is really what God wants us to do. That is what we mean by discernment of God's will. It requires great detachment, prayer and self-denial. If our project is God's will, we will have the power of the Spirit for its accomplishment; if it is not God's will, the Holy Spirit will not empower us for its accomplishment.

We must never take the sanctifying gift of the Spirit in our hearts for granted. We must constantly cultivate the heart through prayer, contemplation, silence and faithful action. Pope Paul VI had a timely reflection. He said:

the Holy Spirit's presence in individual souls can diminish or be missing entirely. This is why the word of God is preached and the sacraments of grace are distributed; this is why people pray and why each individual tries to merit the great 'Gift of God', the Holy Spirit, for himself and for the whole Church.[9]

Empowering Presence of the Spirit

The Spirit also dwells in our hearts for the sake of others. We are witnesses to the risen Christ, servants of the Kingdom of God. Just as Jesus, in the state of human weakness, did not proclaim the Gospel and witness to the Kingdom before he was empowered by the Holy Spirit, so we cannot witness to the Kingdom before we receive that same empowerment. That is why Jesus told his first disciples not to leave Jerusalem 'until you are clothed with power from on high'.

This empowerment is not for our sanctification, but for our mission. For our sanctification we need the indwelling presence of the Holy Spirit in our hearts; for our mission we need the power of the Holy Spirit in our ministry. We call the empowering presence of the Holy Spirit in our lives 'charismatic grace'. Sanctifying grace is given to us by the Spirit for our personal union with God; charismatic grace is given to us by the same Spirit for our mission or ministry in the Church.

Jesus promises us both the sanctifying and the empowering presence of the Spirit. It is true to say that for a long time the Church has been so concerned about the sanctifying presence of the Spirit that she tended to neglect the empowering presence of the Spirit. Indeed, one could argue the case that for many centuries we have not really expected the Spirit to empower us with those charismatic graces with which he empowered the first Christians.

For years I led Christian communities in the Easter Vigil. When I proclaimed the words 'Jesus Christ, the same yesterday, today, and forever' (Heb 13.8) the question would always come to my mind: if this is true, why is Jesus not doing the same things today as he did among his first followers? I would answer myself in this way: Jesus is forgiving sins and sanctifying people today and that is the real work of salvation. That was my way of avoiding the challenge of the Easter proclamation. Jesus Christ is the same for us as he was for the first followers in Jerusalem. He is present to us with the same divine compassion and mercy. He wants us to have the same experience of his forgiving and healing presence as Peter and Paul had.

We have, however, 'over-spiritualized' the work of Christ. We began to see his work in terms of the 'salvation of the soul' and not in terms of the 'salvation of the whole person'. This aberration may have been due to the inculturation of the Gospel in the dominant culture of the Roman Empire. This culture was dominated by Platonic philosophy.

Plato died four hundred years before Christ. For Plato the human person is a composite of body and soul. The soul is immortal and the body is mortal. The early Christian apologists and theologians were able to identify with this philosophy. The human soul is immortal. Death is not the end. Christian thinkers began to teach and defend the faith through the philosophical language of their time. They became Christian Platonists. The necessary process of the inculturation of the Gospel had begun. The Church began to think and speak through the language of the people, using the ideas and the concepts and the images of the people.

Not all aspects of Plato's view of the composition of the human person were, however, compatible with the Christian vision. For Plato, the soul is in the body as in a prison. He had what we call 'a dualistic view' – soul and body were at war with each other. The happiest day in the life of the soul is when the war is ended, through death, and the soul is released from the body.

Plato did not have much time for the body. It was flesh, corruptible and mortal. The soul was spiritual, incorruptible and immortal. Only the soul really mattered. Strains of dualism have survived the centuries!

If we believe that death is a happy release of the soul from the prison of the body, we may logically begin to conclude that anything which causes death, such as sickness, is a good thing. And, indeed, this attitude towards sickness developed in the Church. Sickness was even called 'a time of divine visitation'. Of course, if sickness is caused by God it would not be right to pray against it. We don't pray against what God is doing! Consequently, we don't pray for healing.

This new attitude to sickness had serious pastoral impli-

cations. The emphasis changed from the healing ministry
to a spirituality of suffering. Sickness was a time of 'divine
visitation'. The sick person should be encouraged to offer
up the sufferings. Even the sacrament of the sick took on a
new meaning. It ceased to be primarily a sacrament for
those who were sick and in need of healing and became the
sacrament of 'the last anointing', Extreme Unction. The
sick person would not receive this sacrament until the very
final stages of illness. The anointing became so associated
with dying that many people conceived a great fear of the
sacrament. Even to this day some relatives will ask the priest
not to speak to a very sick person about 'the last rites'!

The whole focus was on the salvation of the soul. The
healing and restoration of the body were not considered.
Even though they were never explicitly denied, they were
not expected. The result? We spiritualized the healing ministry of Jesus and saw it more in terms of the forgiveness
of sins. Since Jesus continues to forgive sins today we were
happy to accept our Easter proclamation that he is indeed
the same yesterday, today and forever. Despite the teaching
of the Council of Trent, which explicitly stated that 'sometimes sickness is healed' through anointing, the general
faith expectation saw anointing only as the preparation for
death.

Along with this over-spiritualization of the healing ministry of Jesus and the inordinate focus on 'the soul' to the
detriment of 'the body', we had a waning of the charisms
in the Church. But in the first three centuries we find the
Church, in the midst of persecution, vigorous and strong
in the Spirit. The gifts of the Spirit, especially the gift of
healing, were prevalent. I will cite just a few witnesses from
those early centuries.

Justin Martyr, a convert philosopher, writing around the

year 165 AD to the Roman Emperor, pleading on behalf of
the Christians, stated:

> For numberless demoniacs throughout the world, and in
> your own city, many of our Christian men exorcising
> them in the name of Jesus Christ . . . have healed and
> do heal, rendering helpless and driving the possessing
> demons out of them, though they could not be cured by
> all the other exorcists, and those who used incantations
> and drugs.

Later on in the second century Tertullian, an African
lawyer, writing to the Roman Proconsul of North Africa
during a period of persecution, reminded him of these facts:

> And how many men of rank have been delivered from
> devils, and healed of diseases! Even Severus himself, the
> father of Antonine [the Emperor] was graciously mindful
> of the Christians; for he sought out the Christian
> Proculus . . . and in gratitude for his having once cured
> him by anointing, he kept him in his palace till the day
> of his death.

In the following century the great theologian Origen, writing around the year 253 AD stated: 'And the name of Jesus
can still remove distractions from the minds of men, and
expel demons, and also take away diseases; and produce a
marvellous meekness of spirit and a complete change of
character'.[10]

From these three reliable witnesses we can see that in
those first three centuries the promise of Christ was fulfilled. His disciples did the same works that he himself did.
In fact it was by doing the works of Christ, healing the sick

and casting out evil spirits that those first Christians had the opportunity to bring the good news of Christ to the pagans who were persecuting them.

I often asked myself how the Christians of those first three centuries managed to convert so many people, all over the pagan Roman Empire, despite the fact that they were an illegal body, persecuted, without any rights of assembly, and without any public means of communication. The historian of the ancient Roman Empire, Ramsey Mac-Mullan has studied this very question. He tries to imagine what openings the Christians had for converting pagans. He writes:

> I would choose a room of a sick person; there, a servant talking to a mistress, or one spouse to another, saying, perhaps, 'Unquestionably they can help, if you believe'. And I know, I have seen . . . they have related to me, they have books, they have a special person, a sort of officer. It is true . . . they can help even in great sickness. I know people who have seen or who have spoken to others who have seen. And healing is even the least that they tell. Theirs is truly a God all-powerful. He has worked a hundred wonders. . . . So, a priest is sent for, or an exorcist; illness is healed; the household after that counts itself Christian; it is baptised; and through instruction it comes to accept the first consequence: that all other cults are false and wicked and all seeming gods, the same.[11]

In this view it was the healing ministry which spearheaded the early Church's evangelistic successes. Those early Christians set out not just to heal the sick and drive out demons in the name of Jesus. They set out to demonstrate that Jesus Christ alone was Lord and Saviour and that all the other gods of the pagans were worthless and powerless idols. St Antony the Hermit is a good example of this technique.

Antony lived in solitude in the desert for forty years. He attracted thousands of followers. Two pagan philosophers, who had lost students to Antony, went into the desert to debate with him. St Athanasius, in his life of Antony, relates what happened.

> Antony said to them 'we convince because people first trust what they actually see, and then in reasoned argument' and Antony added 'look now: here are some folk suffering from daimones . . . either cleanse these men by your logic-chopping or by any other skill or magic you wish, and calling on your idols, or, otherwise, if you can't lay down your quarrel with us and witness the power of Christ's cross'. And with these words he called on Christ, sealed the sufferers with the sign of the cross twice and a third time, and straightaway the men stood forth all healed.[12]

In those early centuries, when the Church was suffering persecutions, the disciples continued to evangelize in the same way as Jesus did. They healed the sick, they cast out evil spirits, they brought people to an experience of the Lordship of Jesus. In the words of St Mark 'the Lord worked with them confirming the word by the signs that accompanied it' (Mk 16.20). Then the Emperor Constantine made peace with the Church in the year 313 AD. He himself became a Christian and richly endowed the Church. The religious situation was transformed. The Church now had the protection of the mighty empire.

Constantine wanted the Church and State to live and work in harmony.

Following the 'peace of Constantine' a marked decline in the manifestation of the charisms of the Spirit seems to have taken place. Some began to find the reason for this decline, not in any decline of expectant faith, but in the plan of God himself. They developed the theory that God gave the gifts of the Spirit at the beginning of the Church, for the preaching of the Gospel 'to the ends of the earth'. In the ancient Roman world Spain was deemed to be the ends of the earth. There was a growing conviction that the Church had fulfilled its mandate to bring the Gospel to the whole world. The gifts of the Spirit, which were given for this purpose, were no longer needed and consequently God had withdrawn them!

Very few would ascribe to this theory, known as *dispensationalism*, today. Yet that theory held sway in the Church for nearly sixteen hundred years, right up to the Second Vatican Council. The Council happily restated the teaching of the Church on the role of charisms in the life of the Church and the sanctification of God's people. I will quote in full the main text:

It is not only through the sacraments and the ministrations of the Church that the Holy Spirit makes holy the People, leads them and enriches them with virtues. Allotting his gifts according as he wills (cf. 1 Cor 12.11) he also distributes special graces among the faithful of every rank. By these gifts he makes them fit and ready to undertake various tasks and offices for the renewal and the building up of the Church, as it is written 'the manifestation of the Spirit is given to everyone for profit' (1 Cor 12.7). Whether these charisms be very remarkable or more simple and widely diffused, they are to be received with thanksgiving and consolation since they are fitting and useful for the needs of the Church.[13]

Since the Council's clear and prophetic teaching on the role of the charisms we have had the experience of 'charismatic renewal in the Church'. This renewal in the Spirit has brought the experience of the gifts of the Spirit, the gift of tongues, healings, deliverance, and many other gifts to millions of Christians all over the world.

We have witnessed the emergence of the lay ministries in the Church. Men and women, from all walks of life, have discovered that they have gifts of the Spirit for serving the community of the faithful.

We have also witnessed great renewal in parish life. In our parish of St Mary's, Clapham, I have observed over the past five years great renewal in the Spirit. Very many of our parishioners have become hungry for the Word of God. They meet in 'cells' to share their faith, to listen to God's Word, to reach out to those who do not, as yet, believe in the Lord Jesus. They want to be evangelists of Christ. On parish missions I have met the same hunger for the Word of God, the same longing to become involved in the mission of the Church, in hundreds of men and women. With such a movement of the Spirit we must surely hope that the Church, especially in the parishes, will be renewed in our time.

Some observers often sound a pessimistic note when they look at the Church because of the diminishing numbers of vocations and the decreasing and ageing Sunday congregations. I would have to say, on the contrary, that in my experience the Church is far more alive today than in the 1950s, and 1960s, when we had much larger numbers.

God is clearly renewing his Church, pouring out the gifts of the Spirit in abundance and gifting many people with new ministries.

One of the most significant gifts which the Spirit is reviving in the Church today is the gift of *inner healing*. Jesus said that he came so that we might have 'Life in abundance'. The gift of inner healing enables the Church to minister to the inner person, to heal the inner wounds and hurts which impede the abundant life which the Lord wants to give.

This ministry is for the whole Church. It is not restricted to priests or ordained ministers. In the next chapter we will consider inner healing as the great service which each of us can render to others, helping them into the experience of 'life in abundance'.

4

Life in Abundance:
Christ's Promise

Speaking about his mission Jesus said 'I have come so that they may have life and have it to the full' (Jn 10.10). Fullness of life, life in abundance; that is Christ's wish for us.

The experience of this abundant life is impeded each time we fail to live by the Word of God. In the hour of his temptation in the desert Jesus proclaimed that 'man does not live on bread alone, but on every word that comes from the mouth of God' (Mt 4.4). Fullness of life cannot be achieved by living on riches, or power, or position. It can only be achieved by living on the Word of God. Once lost, through sin or the wounds of sin, fullness of life can only be restored by that Word of God.

Speaking about the centrality of his Word in the life of the disciples Jesus said: 'If you make my word your home you will indeed be my disciples, you will learn the truth and the truth will make you free' (Jn 8.31). Most people know the phrase 'the truth will make you free'. Sometimes people mistakenly look to the blunt speaking of the truth as the best way of serving freedom. They miss the whole context of what Jesus said.

I remember once taking this word 'the truth will make

you free' very seriously. I said to myself, this is the secret
of life. I want to be free. All I have to do is speak the truth
and do the truth and then I will be free. I went at it with
the zeal of a novice, but soon I discovered that, at least in
my case, it didn't seem to work. When I spoke the truth to
people, as I saw it, I didn't always set them free. And
when people spoke the truth to me, as they saw it, they
didn't always set me free either. In fact, very often the
opposite was happening. I was finding resentments and
anger coming, instead of freedom. I was saying to myself:
'What does Jesus really mean? This is God's Word! It should
be an efficacious Word'. Then one day I was reading the
whole passage again. I was amazed at the words I had never
noticed. Jesus did not simply say 'the truth will make you
free'. He laid down very precise conditions, which must be
fulfilled, before the truth achieves the power to make us
free. The first condition is this: '*if you make my word your
home*'. I had missed that. Some place must be home for
mind and heart. The homeless mind would be even more
distressing than the homeless body. Jesus invites us to make
his word our home. Home is the place where you feel 'at
your ease'. You can be yourself because you know who you
are. Home gives you your identity as son or daughter of
the house.

Jesus says that if we make his Word our home we will
receive a new identity: '*you will be my disciples*'. This is the
second condition which must be fulfilled before the truth
can make us free. I had missed that also. We are either
disciples of Jesus or disciples of some other master. And,
as Jesus himself said, 'we cannot serve two masters'. Pope
John Paul II in his great encyclical on Christian morality
describes what is involved in discipleship in this way: 'it
involves *holding fast to the very person of Jesus*, partaking of

his life and destiny, sharing in his free and loving obedience to the Father. By responding in faith and following the one who is Incarnate Wisdom, the disciple of Jesus truly becomes a *disciple of God* (Jn 6.45)'.[1] By identifying with Christ, in this total and personal way, we receive our new identity as his disciples.

The third condition which must be fulfilled before the truth has the power to make us free is this: '*you will learn the truth*'. I had missed that also. I thought I knew the truth. The truth which makes us free is the truth which we are willing to learn, as disciples, dwelling in the Word of Jesus as in our home.

The truth about our life and destiny is contained in the Word of Christ. The Church of Christ, 'which upholds the truth and keeps it safe' (1 Tim 3.14), interprets his Word for us. As the Vatican Council said, 'The task of authentically interpreting the word of God, whether in its written form or in that of Tradition, has been entrusted only to those charged with the Church's living Magisterium, whose authority is exercised in the name of Jesus Christ'.[2] Christ alone is our teacher. His teaching comes to us through his Church. Dwelling in Christ's Word, as in our home, will always involve dwelling in the Church of Christ, his body on earth. The truth which we will learn, dwelling in the Word of Jesus, is the truth about God and about our relationship with God. That is the truth which will make us free.

As we live on every word that comes from the mouth of God we will learn the truth about ourselves and we will come into the freedom of the children of God. We live on some word about ourselves. We must choose either God's Word or what Scripture calls 'the destructive word' (Ps 52.4). The destructive word is the sinful word, the very opposite of the creative Word. The destructive word is the lie about ourselves. If we live the lie about ourselves, instead of living the truth about ourselves, we will have no freedom or peace.

Jesus compares his Word, God's Word, to a house. We can take up our residence in that house. There is also another word identified in Scripture where we can take up our residence. This is the 'destructive word'. We read 'you love the destructive word' (Ps 52.3). We have, then, the image of two houses where we can make home, the house of the creative Word of God or the house of the destructive word. We form our self-image in one of those houses.

Formation of Self-image

The self-image resides in our subconscious. It controls the way we *feel* about ourselves. We are not born with a self-image: it is formed by the word that is spoken to us. Ultimately we have to say that the self-image is formed either by the Word of God or by the destructive word.

If we have made our home in the house of the creative Word of God we will have a good self-image; if, however, we have made our home in the house of the destructive word we will have a poor self-image. We will feel bad about ourselves and, as a result, we will feel bad about others.

Our self-image must be formed by the Word of God. In every eventuality of life there is a Word of God to live on. Entering into freedom, growing in our freedom, maintaining and protecting our freedom, will not happen if we do not faithfully live each day on Christ's Word. As Pope John Paul said, 'The Crucified Christ reveals the authentic meaning of freedom; he lives it fully in the total gift of himself and calls his disciples to share in his freedom'.[3]

Inner Healing

Using the image of the house of the creative Word and the house of the destructive word we can say that the ministry of inner healing consists in enabling a person to move out of the latter and take up residence in the former. The first step in inner healing is to help the person hear the Word of God and live on it.

Inner healing can be defined in this way: An experience of the healing love of God in which the person realizes that self is lovable (healing of self-image) or that he or she is capable of loving and forgiving (healing of relationships) or that he or she can gratefully integrate some past event into the present (healing of memories).

Healing the Self-image

It is always prudent to begin a ministry of inner healing with prayer for the healing of the self-image. If the self-image is not formed by the Word of God it will be deformed by the destructive word. A deformed self-image would be a great barrier to other forms of inner healing.

The first step in this ministry is the proclamation of God's Word that the person is a beloved child of God. We help the person, through listening prayer, to get out of the house of the destructive word and take up residence in the house of the creative Word.

If our self-image is formed in the house of the creative Word of God it will correspond to how God himself sees us. We must see ourselves as God sees us. We do not have to guess at how God sees us; he himself tells us. The whole Bible is a long love letter which God has written to us. In the very first chapter God tells us the model he had in mind when he created us: 'let us make man in our own image, in the likeness of ourselves' (Gen 1.26). The first thing God reveals to us is that we are like God. God's image and likeness! God's creative love made us like himself. God declared that we are 'very good' (Gen 1.31).

Then the mysterious reality of sin infected God's good creation. We cut ourselves off from God. Adam and his wife, we are told, 'hid from Yahweh God among the trees of the garden' (Gen 3.8). When challenged by God, Adam said, 'I heard the sound of your voice in the garden. I was afraid because I was naked, so I hid' (Gen 3.11). Adam had fallen from the paradise of God-consciousness into the pain of self-consciousness. In this new consciousness he rejected himself. He could no longer accept himself as he was. So he hid. He had alienated himself from God, but also he had rejected himself. He was ashamed. God came looking for him: 'Where are you?' (Gen 3.9). It is always God who comes looking for us. When we sin we hide ourselves away from God. God calls to us, 'Where are you?' That call of God has followed humankind down through the centuries.

God will not allow us to hide away in our shame. He wants us to live without fear in his presence. So he reassures us in our fallen state:

> Do not be afraid, for I have redeemed you;
>   I have called you by your name, you are mine . . .
> Because you are precious in my eyes,
>   because you are honoured and I love you . . .
> Do not be afraid, for I am with you.
>
>   Isaiah 43.2, 4

God's redeeming love reaches its fulfilment in Christ. God

became a human being like us in Christ. He entered into our weakness and sinfulness. Indeed, he took all our sinfulness on himself and redeemed us:

> We had all gone astray like sheep,
>   each taking his own way,
> and Yahweh burdened him
> with the sins of all of us.
>   Isaiah 53.6

Christ has redeemed us from our 'fallen state'. In the words of the Vatican Council, 'By his incarnation, he, the son of God, has in a certain way united himself with each man'.[4] Christ unites us to himself. He has lifted us up out of our fallen self-consciousness and given us a Christ-consciousness. Now when we become aware of ourselves we can become aware of ourselves in union with Christ. We are not on our own. Christ lives in us. As the Vatican Council said, 'In reality it is only in the mystery of the Word made flesh that the mystery of man truly becomes clear'.[5]

In his first encyclical letter Pope John Paul II wrote:

The man who wishes to understand himself thoroughly – and not just in accordance with the immediate, partial, often superficial, and even illusory standards and measures of his being – he must with all his unrest, uncertainty and even his weakness and sinfulness, with his life and death, draw near to Christ. He must, so to speak, enter into him with his own self, he must 'appropriate' and assimilate the whole reality of the Incarnation and the Redemption in order to find himself. If this profound process takes place within him, he then bears fruit not only in adoration of God but also of deep wonder at himself'.[6]

In this magnificent passage the Pope gives us the whole theology of the ministry of inner healing, viz. 'appropriating and assimilating the whole reality of the Incarnation and Redemption'. He goes on to clarify and specify the Church's ministry in this way:

> The Church wishes to serve this single end: that each person may be able to find Christ, in order that Christ may walk with each person the path of life, with the power of the truth about man and the world that is contained in the mystery of the Incarnation and the Redemption and with the power of love that is radiated by that truth.[7]

The ministry of inner healing consists, then, in helping the person to 'appropriate and assimilate the mystery of the Incarnation and the Redemption'.

The healing of the self-image will begin when the person comes to the realization that he or she is united to Christ and that all the grace and merit of Christ become his or her own through faith and conversion. As St Paul said: 'For anyone who is in Christ there is a new creation; the old creation is gone, the new one is here. It is all God's work' (2 Cor 5.17). The ministry of inner healing seeks to bring the person to that realization.

To sum up, the ministry begins with the Word of God. The person must hear the invitation of Jesus: 'if you make my word your home'. Inner healing begins as the person begins to learn the truth about self, the truth that he or she is precious in God's sight. That is the word the person must live on.

Self-acceptance

Self-rejection is the first fruit of sin. Like Adam, the sinner seeks to hide himself from the presence of God. He fears God, because he feels that his sin has robbed him of all dignity in the presence of God. He loses the sense of what the Vatican Council called 'man's surpassing dignity'.[8] He finds it very hard to pray. Even if he 'says his prayers' he will not feel comfortable in the divine presence.

A priest was sent by his bishop to Hawkstone Hall, the Redemptorist International Pastoral and Renewal Centre for priests, religious and laity in Shropshire, while I was director.[9] His problem was he could not pray. He was a young active parish priest and had succeeded an old man who had been parish priest for thirty-five years. During those years the Vatican Council never happened in his parish! Now this young, dynamic priest takes over. He does all that a modern parish priest should be doing. The people are delighted and are singing his praises. But he himself is not praying. The praises of the people are getting to him. He is feeling a real hypocrite and is in danger of a breakdown. He arrived at Hawkstone Hall in a state of tension and confusion.

When I heard that his real problem was that he could not pray (he was saying all the prescribed prayers) I asked him to read out the first ten verses of Isaiah 43. When he came to the verse 'because you are precious in my eyes' I asked him to respond. He said with great vehemence, 'he is not referring to me'. That was his problem with prayer:

he felt that God had a very high opinion of everyone else but entertained a very low opinion of himself!

I gave him a simple exercise. I asked him to join the course (there were around seventy priests and religious on a three-month renewal course) at the Holy Hour each evening and simply say, 'Jesus, I thank you that I am precious in your Father's sight'.

He told me afterwards that he felt very foolish on the first evening. He would look around from time to time and see all the others lost in prayer and contemplation and there he was, wringing his hands and forcing himself to say 'Jesus, I thank you that I am precious in your Father's sight'. But he persevered with the prayer. And in three days that man was so full of prayer that he couldn't stop praying. He was spending hours in the church, singing hymns all over the place, and, in general, living a whole new God experience. What had happened? He had begun to live on the Word of God. He had vacated the house of the destructive word, in which he felt no good, and taken up residence in the house of the creative Word, where he heard that he was precious in God's sight.

He began to accept himself. He discovered the truth of Guardini's remark: 'The act of self-acceptance is the root of all things. I must agree to be the person who I am. Agree to have the qualifications which I have. Agree to live within the limitations set for me. . . . The clarity and the courageousness of this acceptance is the foundation of all existence'.[10] Self-acceptance is the goal of Christian existence. It is not there by birth, but by our rebirth. As St Peter said, 'your new birth was not from any mortal seed but from the everlasting word of the living and eternal God' (1 Peter 1.23). My self-acceptance is not based on my own merits; it is based on God's Word to me, on God's acceptance of me. The divine acceptance makes self-acceptance possible. It is a work of grace, the fruit of redemption.

The act of self-acceptance must be fortified by prayer and the determination to live on the Word of God. Scripture teaches us to pray this prayer of self-acceptance:

> It was you who created my inmost self,
>   who put me together in my mother's womb;
> for all these mysteries I thank you:
> for the wonder of myself, for the wonder
> of your works.
>
> Ps 139.12–13

We must not only pray this prayer, 'I thank you for the wonder of myself', but we must live it. Inner healing comes to the self-image when we gratefully thank God each day for the wonder of ourselves.

God delights in holding a dialogue with us. He says to us 'you are precious in my eyes' and he awaits our reply. That Word of God is an everlasting word spoken over each of us. God does not have to repeat it. We are already addressed by God even before we turn to him in prayer. We have to respond to his Word. It is spoken over us and remains over us forever. The Holy Spirit has given us this beautiful psalm for a fitting reply. Because we are precious in God's sight we can thank him for the wonder of ourselves!

Speaking about 'appropriating and assimilating the whole reality of the Incarnation and Redemption', Pope John Paul II concluded:

> if this profound process takes place within him, he then bears fruit not only of adoration of God but also of deep

wonder at himself. How precious must man be in the
eyes of the Creator, if he 'gained so great a Redeemer'
and if God 'gave his only Son' in order that man should
not perish but have eternal life.[11]

This prayer of self-acceptance is the first step on the road
to the healing of the self-image: growing in wonder at one's
own dignity as a child of God. The prayer is the opposite
of the sin. Sin causes alienation from self; sin fills the person
with guilt and shame; sin may even instil a deep self-hatred.
This prayer, on the other hand, fills the person with gratitude for God's wonderful creation. It opens the human
spirit to rejoice in the Holy Spirit. It prepares the heart for
a deeper, ongoing conversion. The more we fill ourselves
with gratitude to God for the wonder of ourselves the more
we will reject everything which is contrary to our dignity.
    We cannot sustain for very long these two contrary modes
of action, viz. thanking God for the wonder of ourselves
while at the same time attacking our own dignity by sinful
behaviour. Such a way of behaving would create in us what
psychologists call 'cognitive dissonance', that is an
emotional state when two simultaneously held attitudes or
beliefs are inconsistent or when there is a conflict between
belief and behaviour. The healing of the self-image comes
about through creating this 'cognitive dissonance'. The
person is feeling bad about self, feeling worthless. Then he
begins to pray, 'I thank you for the wonder of myself'. This
creates the healthy conflict between what he professes in
prayer and what he feels in himself. By persevering with
the prayer the bad feelings about self will begin to change.
Instead of experiencing self-rejection or even self-hatred he
will come into a new self-acceptance and a new gratitude
for self.

The healing of the self-image is a process and it takes time. The key to this healing is *listening* to the Word of God. If a person is not willing to listen to God's Word there is no basis for healing. On the other hand, if the person is willing to listen to God's Word, willing to live on his Word, there is no wound in the self-image which will not be healed.

While working with a group of religious at Hawkstone I once asked the sister sitting next to me if she would be the first to introduce herself and tell the group why she had come on the course. She was seized with panic and had great difficulty in speaking. We all felt very sorry for her. After the session I talked to her about inner healing and promised her that she could be completely healed from this panic. She told me that the panic was there because when she was about twelve her teacher had made her stand before the whole class to do a sum which she didn't know. He called her a stupid girl and then got one of the boys to do the sum on the blackboard. That cruel remark robbed her of all self-confidence. She suffered intensely each time she had to speak in public; she could never read in public. Even though she was a highly qualified nurse, a ward sister, she felt totally inadequate in public.

She received the teaching on inner healing as good news. Each morning she would thank God for the wonder of herself and for all her good gifts. I asked her group to pray with her frequently, asking the Lord to take from her deep subconscious the word 'stupid' and fill her whole being with the words 'precious in my sight'. Before the course was over she not only read during Mass but she also wrote a wonderful poem and recited it to the whole course. She was living now on the Word of God, which declared that she was precious, and not on the word of the teacher, which declared that she was stupid. Her self-image had been healed and her confidence restored.

Healing of Relationships

The heartfelt prayer of Jesus at the Last Supper was for unity among his disciples: 'With me in them and you in me, may they be so completely one that the world will realise that it was you who sent me' (Jn 17.23). Jesus prays that the unity of his disciples will mirror on earth the unity of the Trinity in heaven. Such a unity can only come from God. This divine gift of unity was given to the Church. The Vatican Council, quoting the great martyr St Cyprian, said the universal Church is 'a people brought into unity from the unity of the Father, the Son and the Holy Spirit'.[12]

God wills that the multiplicity of our relationships is enriched with love and unity. 'God is love and anyone who lives in love lives in God, and God lives in him' (1 Jn 4.17). Disunity is not the hallmark of God's work. Unity is the fruit of grace and love; disunity is the bitter fruit of sin and selfishness. We have, regrettably, disunity: in the Church; in the home; in the extended family; among friends. Human relationships, the source of so much joy, when they are enriched with love and unity, become the source of bitter pain, when they are distorted through disunity and lack of love. But God heals broken relationships through the gift of forgiving love. St Peter asked Jesus about forgiveness: ' "Lord how often must I forgive my brother if he wrongs me? As often as seven times?" Jesus answered, "Not seven, I tell you, but seventy-seven times" ' (Mt 18.21).

Jesus is saying to Peter that the quality of Christian forgiveness is *unconditional*. There are no limits. It is not a question of 'How often must I forgive?'; rather, forgiveness itself becomes the very sign of my Christian existence. No forgiveness, no Christian life! Jesus concludes his parable of the unforgiving debtor with these words: 'And that is how my heavenly Father will deal with you unless you each forgive your brother from your heart' (Mt 18.35). Forgiveness is never a question of 'meeting the other person half way', nor is it a question of forgiving 'provided he doesn't do it again'. Christian forgiveness lays down no conditions. It goes all the way, all the time.

Christian forgiveness, then, must be seen as an act of divine love. We are not capable of that kind of forgiveness by our own powers. It is Christ in us who enables us to forgive in this Christlike way. Jesus reminded us, 'without me you can do nothing'. Without Christ, without the sincere desire to live the life of Christ, we cannot forgive unconditionally. But when we do forgive we become like God himself. 'Be compassionate as your heavenly Father is compassionate' (Lk 6.36); compassionate forgiveness makes us like God himself. In the very act of forgiving we radiate God's image and likeness.

People frequently misunderstand the nature of forgiveness. They confuse forgiveness with condoning the wrong done or excusing the fault or crime of another. Forgiveness, in fact, is the very opposite of condoning or excusing. As C. S. Lewis wrote:

There is all the difference in the world between forgiving and excusing. Forgiveness says, 'Yes, you have done this thing, but I accept your apology, I will never hold it against you and everything between us two will be exactly the same as it was before'. But excusing says, 'I see that you couldn't help it, or didn't mean it, you weren't really to blame'. If one was not really to blame then there is nothing to forgive. In that sense forgiveness and excusing are almost opposite.[13]

When I say to someone 'I forgive you' I am saying that the person has wronged me and that he or she had no excuse. But I am also saying that, because I am a child of the forgiving Father in heaven, I forgive in imitation of his forgiveness. I forgive because God forgives me. This is the great grace of forgiveness. In forgiving I become like God!

When I ask myself why God demands that we should forgive the person who wrongs us, the words of the psalm come to mind: 'The Law of Yahweh is perfect, new life to the soul' (Ps 19.7). Forgiveness brings 'new life to the soul' because forgiveness sets us free from those who hurt us.

Consider what happens within you when someone hurts you. You can spend the whole day thinking about the hurt. The person who hurt you can be in your thoughts night and day. You can become preoccupied with the person. Each time you think of him or her you experience the hurt afresh. Indeed, if the hurt was really deep, the person seems to have the power to haunt you. As one lady colourfully expressed it to me, 'I am carrying him [her estranged husband] around in my head, rent free, twenty-four hours a day! I would love to get rid of him out of my mind'. I gave her this image to work with: unforgiveness is like putting your two hands around a person's throat and holding tight. As long as you hold the person by the throat you will be seeing that person right in front of you. The only way to get rid of the person is to open your hands and let go. She wanted to let go.

Forgiveness, then, is letting go. Unforgiveness holds you in bondage to the person who has hurt you. Forgiveness breaks that bondage. Forgiveness sets you free. 'The Law of the Yahweh is perfect, new life for the soul.' As soon as that lady entered into forgiveness she experienced a new freedom and got her estranged husband 'out of her mind'.

Because forgiveness is a divine gift it has the power 'to bind up hearts that are broken' (Isaiah 61.1). When someone you have loved 'breaks your heart' what can you do? From the pain of the broken heart you can seek revenge. You can curse the person and wish him or her all kinds of evil. Or you can take the path of freedom and forgive. Forgiveness is at the heart of the Gospel: it is not just one Christian attitude among many others. It sums up in itself the whole mystery of salvation. Because God has forgiven me, I can forgive others. When God forgives me, his forgiveness remains within me. It becomes the source of my power to forgive. Without God's forgiveness in my own life I am powerless to forgive others.

The person who has been deeply hurt has to hear the good news of forgiveness. The hurt can become the occasion of a whole new experience of the power of God. An example will illustrate this. During a parish mission in a certain city I was helped greatly by the lady who looked after the church. She was there before all the services to make sure that I had everything I needed. One afternoon, towards the end of the mission, I unexpectedly met her in the church. She was telling me how well the mission was going. I said to her, half jokingly, 'I hope you have got the big blessing yourself'. Her whole attitude changed at once and she said with an astonishing degree of sarcasm, 'If you mean that business of honouring your father and mother that you were talking about last night you'd better forget it!'

I was quite taken aback. I knew she was a devout believer. Such a remark had to come from some very deep hurt

within her. She saw the look of puzzlement on my face and
she added, 'If you came through what I came through you
would not be surprised at what I have just said'. I was
praying hard for her because for the first time I recognized
that she was in great need of help. It was, I felt, a moment
of grace for her.

Reluctantly, she began to tell me her story. When she
was one day old her mother put her in a cardboard box
and left her on the steps of a church. It was a Saturday
night, in the middle of winter. As the lady who was doing
the flowers for Sunday morning came out of the church
she saw the box and passed on. Then she heard a cry from
the box and turned back. Inside was the little one-day-old
baby, perishing with the cold. She not only saved the baby's
life but she also adopted her as her own daughter. Now the
lady was married herself and had a lovely family. But every
time she hears the words 'honour your father and your
mother' she is gripped with a totally uncharacteristic hardness and coldness. 'You wouldn't expect me to honour a
woman like that, would you?' she challengingly said to me.
I had the presence of mind to say, 'No, I wouldn't, but I
know God does, and if God wants you to honour your
mother, God gives you the power to do so.'

After talking about her experience for some time she
agreed to my offer of prayer. I invited her to come to the
foot of the cross and to listen to Jesus praying for those
who were crucifying him. She knew the prayer well: 'Father,
forgive them, for they don't know what they are doing'. I
asked her to listen deeply to that prayer. She did. Then
I asked her if she would like Jesus to say that prayer for her
mother. She replied, more or less, that Jesus could do what
he liked! But she listened. Then I said to her that I would
like to say the same prayer for her mother and so I began

to repeat the prayer: 'Father, forgive her, she doesn't know what she is doing'. After a while I invited her to say the same prayer herself. At first she adamantly refused; then she began to waver, and finally she joined in the prayer, 'Father, forgive her, she doesn't know what she is doing'. The moment she entered into the prayer of forgiveness she received God's promise: 'I shall give you a new heart, and put a new spirit in you; I shall remove the heart of stone from your bodies and give you a heart of flesh instead. I shall put my spirit in you' (Ezekiel 36.26). All the hardness and coldness were gone. She became grateful to God for her mother and she could once again live on the life-giving Word of God: 'honour your father and mother'.

This woman had come to terms with the tragedy of her abandonment. She had previously convinced herself that the best way forward was never even to think about her mother. She presumed that God's commandment 'honour your father and mother' did not apply to her. It was a new revelation to her of God's great love and forgiveness when he took away her 'heart of stone' and gave her a new heart for her mother. What seemed totally impossible to her became possible in God's power.

By listening humbly to the prayer of Jesus on the cross and seeking to make that prayer her own she was, in the words of Pope Paul II 'appropriating and assimilating the whole reality of the Incarnation and Redemption' and so 'she found herself'. She found herself as a daughter in relation to the mother who had given her birth. And she honoured that mother in her heart.

Jesus had fulfilled his promise, 'I have come to that they may have life and have it to the full'. This abundant life flowed through her as she opened her life to Jesus and sought from him the power to forgive. The power of God's forgiveness is available for the healing of every wounded relationship. How sad, then, when we find people nursing great inner wounds because they either do not know about the liberating power of forgiveness or because they simply refuse to turn to the Lord and ask for that power.

The message of the liberating power of forgiveness is not always welcome even in Christian circles. During a course in an ecumenical institute in the USA on 'The dialogue between psychology and theology', I asked a question about forgiveness and much to my amazement the lecturer, a Christian minister, snapped at me and said, 'I don't go in for cheap forgiveness!' She had been sharing a case with us. She was counselling a female lecturer on the campus, who as a young girl had been brutally sexually abused by her father for several years. She explained the various stages of the therapy and then told us that her next session would be the last one. She had said nothing about forgiveness, nor indeed any other spiritual dimension of the lady's life. It was at this point that I asked at what stage would she speak to the lady about the need to forgive her father. Not only did the lecturer express great indignation but the whole class, all ministers in various churches, shared her anger at my question.

I responded rather heatedly myself and said that I did not speak of 'cheap forgiveness'; I was referring to the forgiveness that comes through the passion and death of Christ, and that was no cheap forgiveness! She then responded to me and said, 'She has nothing to forgive. Her father does not exist anymore'. By this time, the whole class were very angry and the discussion had become less than rational.

Recognizing the strength of opinions on both sides the lecturer then proposed that we should devote the next period, the following week, to forgiveness. During the next session we had a reasonable discussion and sharing on forgiveness as a distinctly Christian response to those who wrong us. At the end of the term, while she was thanking us all for participating in the course, the lecturer said, 'I can guarantee you, this is the only institute in the whole of the USA that has given one hour this term to forgiveness!'

She never gave me a satisfactory answer to this question: How could she, as a Christian minister, bring another Christian woman through a whole course of counselling and refuse to speak to her about the liberating power of Christian forgiveness? I am sure her counselling skills brought some relief to the woman she was helping; Christian forgiveness, however, would have given her a new heart. Forgiveness is like 'laser surgery': no tumour of resentment or hatred can resist it. The minister of Christ who leads a person into forgiveness fulfils the Scripture:

> The spirit of the Lord Yahweh has been given
>   to me,
> for Yahweh has anointed me.
> He has sent me to bring good news to the poor,
> to bind up hearts that are broken.
>
> Isaiah 61.1

Forgiving Oneself

We must extend to ourselves the same forgiveness which we receive from God. I have often heard people declare: 'I will never forgive myself for what I did'. Isn't that a terrible thing to say to oneself? If God forgives us our sins, even our greatest sins, why shouldn't we forgive ourselves? Sin, of course, causes alienation from self. It can even instil hatred and loathing of self. Sin causes self-rejection. Therefore, any unwillingness to forgive oneself may be a sign of a deep root of self-rejection.

After speaking on this subject during a retreat at a top security prison, one man came up to me and said, 'I know exactly what you mean by the need to forgive yourself. I worshipped the ground my wife walked on, but I killed her. I can never forgive myself. I know God forgives me. I am getting out in a month's time. How can I forgive myself?' That man's inner world was shattered. Even though he was deeply repentant he was still living in the house of the destructive word. How could he, a wife killer, be precious in God's sight? After what he had done how could he ever say, 'I thank you for the wonder of myself'?

Among his fellow prisoners there was the man who had been wrongly convicted of a terrible crime, whom I mentioned in the first chapter. This man, whose sentence has since been overturned by the Court of Appeal, had learned the secret of accepting himself, even in his dreadful situation. He was full of the Spirit, free from all bitterness at his unjust sentence. He took that man and ministered to him and brought him into deep peace. He described his experience of the last night of the retreat in this way:

How can I express in words the experience of Sunday evening? We gathered and prayed for the gift of the Holy Spirit in words and singing continuously. It was an experience of great joy. We prayed collectively for the gift of the Spirit for ourselves. Then we went individually to be prayed with. There was a continuous stream of people going up. Everyone was joyfully singing or praying. I could see great joy on the faces of everyone. It was out of this world.

As those prisoners, many of them deeply depressed by bad and bitter memories, opened their hearts to the Lord and forgave themselves, with the same forgiveness they received from the Lord, there was 'great joy on the faces of everyone'. Even the often grim circumstances of prison cannot rob men of the joy of the Lord.

The prisoners discovered the liberating power of forgiveness. First of all we had turned to the Lord for the forgiveness that we all need. Then I had invited them to forgive everyone who had ever hurt them, to share with them the forgiveness they had received. And finally I had asked them to forgive themselves. I asked them to say this prayer: 'Lord I thank you for forgiving me my many sins. Now Lord I forgive myself. I thank you for the wonder of myself. I thank you that I am precious in your sight'.

Every morning we should begin the day with thanking God for the wonder of ourselves; every night, as we examine our conscience and ask pardon of God for the sins of the day, we should also forgive ourselves. That is the way of peace.

Healing of Memories

The experience of Christ's gift of abundant life can be impeded by sad and bitter memories. Memory is a great gift from God. Through memory we can recall all God's gifts. But if memory is abused it becomes a great burden. People can use their memory as a storehouse for resentment, anger and bitterness. As the Scottish poet Robbie Burns would say, 'they nurse their wrath to keep it warm'.

To experience Christ's abundant life we must live on every word that comes from the mouth of God. This is true too of our memory. Scripture tells us how to remember:

> Bless Yahweh, my soul,
> bless his holy name, all that is in me!
> Bless Yahweh, my soul,
> and remember all his kindness.
>
> Ps 103.1–2

The Holy Spirit directs us, in this passage, to bless God, not just with our thoughts and our prayers, but with '*all that is in me*'. What is 'in me'? Everything that has ever happened in my whole life is within me. It is registered in that faculty we call memory. Each experience of life is logged in my internal, personal computer. I cannot consciously remember everything that has ever happened to me at the same time. I recall the different experiences of my life as I need to. I have had hundreds of thousands of experiences last year. They are in my memory. But I am not thinking of them now. However, if I wish, I can go back to some event last February. I can recall how it happened and why, recall how I experienced it at the time; if it was a hurtful event I can feel again the pain it caused; if it was a joyful and affirming event I can relive the joy of that moment.

The hurtful and distressful events of life were bad enough when they happened. They robbed us of peace and joy for some time. If they become painful and resentful memories they can rob us of peace and joy for a lifetime. All those millions of past events have shaped us, action by action. An action from the past can float into our memory, charged with the intensity of resentment or bitterness, and seek to shape our response in the present. That is the power of memory.

The healing of memories is the only effective response to bad memories. Time does not really heal the memory. A person may live for many years without consciously recalling some sad or painful event of the past. Once, however, the painful memory surfaces the person may become sad or depressed or even very angry and resentful. I am sure you may have often been surprised to hear an old person suddenly pour forth bitterness about something which happened many years previously. The passage of time did not take away the bitterness; the memory registered the pain and the bitterness at the time and until that memory is healed the pain and the bitterness remain. In fact we simply talk about the person having painful or bitter memories.

God wants us to have *grateful memories*. Our memories should be patterned on the Holy Eucharist. The Eucharist, the Mass, is the grateful memory of the Church. When he gave us the Eucharist, Jesus said to us, 'do this in memory of me'. In all our eucharistic prayers we specifically remember:

Father, calling to mind the death your Son endured for our salvation, his glorious resurrection and ascension into heaven and ready to greet him when he comes again, we offer you in thanksgiving this holy and living sacrifice.

In the great eucharistic act of remembering we call to mind Christ's Passion, death and Resurrection and we give God praise and glory. We do not call to mind his cruel suffering in order to complain about it or to condemn his tormentors and executioners. We recall to praise God. In the same way we recall our own past sufferings, not to complain or condemn, but to give God glory: 'Bless Yahweh, all that is in me'.

C. S. Lewis said 'praise is inner health made audible'. Past hurts, which fester in the memory as resentments, are healed through the simple prayer of praise: 'Bless Yahweh, all that is in me'. Through acting on this Word of God, resentful memories become grateful memories. I refresh my memory not to complain but to give thanks.

The past is the past. I cannot change it. What I can change is the way I remember the past. I choose to remember resentfully or gratefully. If I remember resentfully the past continues to shape my response in the present. I will be in danger of acting out my resentments. If I meet the person against whom I carry resentments my 'body language' will communicate them. He or she will be made aware that I am resentful and unforgiving. If I remember gratefully, the hurts of the past lose their power to influence my response in the present. I remember not to complain or condemn but to give God thanks. That is how the Christian spirit responds in each situation. St Patrick wrote 'Today, among heathen peoples, I praise and proclaim your name in all places, not only when things go well but also in times of distress. *Whether I receive good or ill, I return thanks equally to God*, who taught me always to trust him unreservedly'.[14] I often think this is the origin of a very typical Irish response to tragedy, 'Sure it could be worse, thank God': I have witnessed people of faith gain enormous strength in the face of some great suffering with those words.

Initially, of course, it may seem impossible to recall and give thanks. The pain may be too great. You must be patient with yourself. If, however, you cannot say 'thanks be to God' as you recall some painful event, what are you saying?

If you are not responding with a blessing you will be responding with a condemnation! And if you are responding with a condemnation, even though you may not formulate it as such, that painful event will remain unintegrated into your being and it will continue to have the power to make you sad or mad.

The grace of the healing of memories brings with it the awareness that I can become grateful for all the events of my past life and integrate them into the present. But I must make the decision. About some past event of my life I am free either to bless or curse. I cannot be saying to myself 'I wish God would do it for me'. God gives me the grace but I must speak the blessing.

As I recall the sinful events of the past I ask God's forgiveness. Then I thank him that in and through the sinful events he was with me and took care of me. This is how the Church, in the great song of the Easter Vigil, thanks God even for the sin of Adam: 'O what a happy fault, O necessary sin of Adam, that gained for us such a great Redeemer'. When we sincerely turn to God even our past sins are occasions for a giving thanks.

As I recall the painful events of the past, the way I hurt myself or the way other people hurt me, I renew my forgiveness and then I thank God that even in and through these unjust and hurtful deeds he was with me. I seek to discern his presence, 'walking the path of life with me', and together we thank God the Father.

I was once leading a parish congregation in this kind of healing prayer, emphasizing that no matter what happened, no matter how sinful or violent it may have been, Christ was present, suffering with the person, supporting and sustaining him or her. After the service a whole family came up to me. They were all crying. The mother spoke for them

all. She said that twelve months previously her 16-year-old
daughter had been murdered. Their greatest pain as a
family was the thought of her being all alone and helpless
as her assassin raped and murdered her. 'Now' she said 'we
know she was not alone. Christ was with her'. They were
at peace in their grief.

That deep realization of Christ being with that young
girl, as she was being brutalized and killed, came to her
family because they were praying 'We thank you Lord that
even in the most distressing situation you are present'. Until
they introduced themselves, I did not know their tragic
history at all. Had I known that they were in the church I
would probably not have focused so much on thanking the
Lord for his presence in all our distressing and sad situ-
ations. But they were obeying God's Word and blessing
God with all that was with them, with the pain and the
agony of the memory of her death, and the gentle realization
that Christ was with her dawned on them and brought
them peace. That is the healing power of the Word of God.

It is not the past event itself which changes, but the way
we remember it. We begin to relate to the past in a new
way. Recalling the past ceases to be the occasion for
experiencing resentment and anger and becomes the
occasion for glorifying God. As we recall and give thanks
the wound in the memory is healed.

Jesus said: 'they are happy who hear the word of God
and keep it'. The Word of God to us about our memory is
'all that is in me bless his holy name'. When we keep this
word, when we live on it, when we really thank God with
'all that is within', we experience the power of God's Word
through the healing of memories. 'He sent forth his word
and he healed them' (Ps 107.20).

I was once praying with a Presbyterian minister who had

very bad memories of his childhood and, as a result, could not forgive or respect his mother. When he was 9 years old, forty years ago, his mother divorced his father and married again. He had to live with his stepfather. The boys at school threw the divorce and second marriage up at him. They mocked him. He felt ashamed of his mother. He eventually became a minister in the Church of Scotland. Yet, despite the fact that he is preaching the Gospel, proclaiming the forgiving love of God, he cannot bring himself to forgive his mother, much less honour her.

As we began to pray I asked him to close his eyes and imagine himself back at home in some familiar situation with his mother and stepfather. He got a clear picture of sitting at the kitchen table with them. Then I asked him to imagine Jesus coming into the kitchen. When he had a clear image of Jesus entering the kitchen I asked him simply to observe what Jesus did and to thank him. We prayed together for some time. I was thanking the Lord for his presence with the family and for his blessing on the family.

When we finished the prayer he was very moved. He told me that when Jesus entered the kitchen he had the clear impression of him sitting down at the table with them. The Lord then took his father's hand and his mother's hand and he placed his father's hand on top of his mother's hand. Then the Lord took his hand and placed it on top of both their hands and held it there. I asked him if that is how he marries a couple and he said yes. He was, in imagination, officiating at the marriage of his parents!

While this symbolic gesture was happening in his imagination, I was thanking the Lord for his presence to and blessing on the family. He realized that all his life he had been condemning his mother for the second marriage; he was ashamed of her second marriage. Now as I began to thank the Lord for his presence in the family he was able to thank God for the second marriage. All the shame was gone. He received a great healing of memory. He said 'I am now going to get into my car and drive straight to see my mother'. He had not seen her for a very long time!

As a footnote to this story it should be said that this minister was an expert counsellor. He was very well versed in the schools of modern psychology. He had come through extensive therapy himself. It was only, however, when he obeyed God's Word and praised God with 'all that is within' that he was delivered from deep shame and healed in his memory.

If there is something painful in your memory and if you really want to be healed, all you have to do is to humbly invite it, whatever it is, to bless God. Hold it patiently before God and say thanks be to God. Once you begin to say 'thanks be to God' over some painful event of the past, the process of the healing of memories has begun. Persevere with this prayer of gratitude, even when you feel you do not or cannot possibly mean it and you will experience in time the healing of your whole memory.

5

Barriers to Inner Healing

St Paul reminded the Thessalonians that the Gospel is 'still a living power among you who believe it' (1 Thess 2.13). In another well-known passage we read, 'the word of God is something alive and active' (Heb 4.12). When we are dealing, then, with the Word of God we must always realize that through this Word the power of God becomes present and active. As Jesus himself says 'the words I have spoken to you are spirit and they are life' (Jn 6.63).

The inner healing ministry shows us that as we take the Word of God seriously, as we begin to live on it and keep it in our heart, we experience its healing and liberating power. In the last chapter we considered three different areas of inner healing, viz. the healing of the self-image, the healing of relationships and the healing of memories. In each area the healing comes through hearing the Word of God and acting on it.

Ministering, then, through the Word of God we have the power to bring people into a new experience of the healing love of God. As we teach people to listen to the Word, to welcome it and respond to it, we see them grow in the Spirit and rejoice in God's healing love. Normally those who sincerely seek inner healing receive it.

If a person is sincerely seeking inner healing, but is not receiving peace, we have to discern what is blocking the peace. There are five major barriers which we will look at: lack of self-acceptance, unrepentance, unforgiveness, guilt, and finally bondage, which we will look at in the next chapter.

Lack of Self-acceptance

We have seen that 'self-acceptance is the root of all things'. It is the root cause of our being at ease with ourselves. Self-rejection, on the other hand, is the root cause of lack of ease, dis-ease, with self. If the person is in the destructive process of rejecting self, inner healing will be blocked.

When the person is not receiving Christ's gift of peace we have to begin a discernment process to investigate whether the cause for the lack of inner healing is a root of self-rejection. We have to keep clearly in mind the counselling principle that the presenting problem is never the real problem. A very good priest once came to me with a big problem. Two of his confreres in community completely ignored him. They would not greet him or acknowledge him. Being a sensitive man he felt very hurt. He also felt worried because he wanted to show them love and forgiveness. He was anxious that, since they were persisting in their coldness towards him, his forgiveness and love might also turn cold. He was convinced that these two men were the big problem in his life. He prayed daily that the Lord would change their hearts. He had others pray with him for the same intention. Still he was worried.

His two confreres were the presenting problem. They were not the real problem. The cause of the real problem was not in them; it was in himself. We had to identify that cause. As he talked about his relationship with them it became clear that, despite his experience of their rejection, he had a daily expectation that one morning they would be glad to see him! In normal human relationships that would be a realistic expectation. But his whole experience of these two men should have told him that it was quite unrealistic for him to expect them to become friendly towards him. In fact, such an expectation was not only unrealistic, it was also laying a great burden on them.

They could not meet his expectation. As a consequence the priest felt rejected and hurt. The prayer that he was receiving for the hurt did not bring peace because the object of the prayer was to get rid of the rejection and not to get rid of his unrealistic expectation. The presenting problem was the rejection; the real problem was his daily, unrealistic expectation that two enemies would become his friends. Once he saw that the cause of the hurt which he was experiencing was not the rejection, but the expectation that the rejection would not happen, he was able to take power over his own life again. He began to see that at the heart of his problem there was a self-rejection.

His self-acceptance was conditional. It depended on his being accepted by others, especially by these two men who were, for their own reasons, unfriendly towards him. By his unrealistic expectation he had given these two men tremendous power over his life. The first step in the healing process for him was not to ask God to change them, but to ask for the grace to withdraw the expectation, to give up the non-verbal demand that they should become friendly towards him.

I shared with him the story of a religious sister who had a similar problem in her community. She had made a directed retreat with me and was experiencing great peace.

There was a sister in her community whom she feared. She said that this sister would disturb her whole peace again in a matter of days! I gave her these simple steps for prayer:

1   Each day thank God for the wonder of herself, then thank God for the wonder of her sister;
2   Thank God for all the good things he is doing in her life, then thank God for all the good things he is doing in her sister's life;
3   Make allowance for all her own failures, as she asked God for pardon, and then make allowance for all her sister's failures.

She told me later that shortly after her return from the retreat this sister said to her one morning, 'You have become very nice to me all of a sudden'!

There is a great lesson in this for all of us. The sister on retreat sincerely felt that this other sister was cold and unfriendly. As a result her 'body language' communicated her fear and apprehension in her presence. She was living in the house of the destructive word in regard to this sister. Then she began to live in the house of the creative Word of God, she began to thank God for the sister and acknowledge all the good things God was doing in her. The 'body language' changed and instead of communicating fear and apprehension she began to communicate acceptance and appreciation.

Again, we see that the presenting problem was not the real problem. The presenting problem was the other sister's apparent coldness; the real problem was that she herself, sensing coldness, was non-verbally communicating her fear and apprehension. God healed this relationship not by changing the other sister but by changing herself. She was unconsciously rejecting herself. She was unhappy, defensive, and apprehensive because her self-acceptance depended on the approval of the other sister. When that was not forthcoming she lost her peace.

If someone has lost heart, if he or she is feeling that the problems of life are too many and too heavy, it is most necessary to help him, in the words of Pope John Paul II, 'to find himself'. The pain, the failures, the sins, the frustrations of life initiate the process of self-rejection. This process is reversed when the person draws near to Christ. As John Paul says,

> he must with all his own unrest, uncertainty and even his weakness and sinfulness, with his life and death, draw near to Christ. He must, so to speak, enter into him with is own self, he must 'appropriate' and assimilate the whole reality of the Incarnation and the Redemption in order to find himself.[1]

The very things which cause self-rejection – namely, sinfulness, weakness, and failure – become the graced opportunity of self-discovery when we bring them all into Christ.

Unrepentance

Sin alienates us from God, from others and from self. The only way to overcome this alienation is through repentance. Sometimes we try to make ourselves believe that we have really repented. As Jeremiah said, 'The heart is more devious than any other thing' (Jer 17.9). If I have sinned and remain unrepentant I will not experience the peace of Christ which comes through inner healing.

In the introduction to the New Rite of Penance we have this description of *metanoia* or repentance:

We can only approach the Kingdom of Christ by *metanoia*. This is a profound change of the whole person by which we begin to consider, judge, and arrange our life according to the holiness and love of God, made manifest in his Son in the last days and given to us in abundance. The genuineness of the penance depends on this heartfelt contrition. For conversion should affect the whole person from within and toward a progressively deeper enlightenment and an ever-closer likeness to Christ.[2]

Metanoia, or conversion, implies 'a profound change of the whole person'. As Bishop Morris Maddocks says, it is 'a reorientation of the whole personality'.[3]

Remorse for sinful behaviour may lead to repentance but it is not in itself repentance. Remorse is the pain of the conscience passing judgement on the sinful action; repentance enables the person 'to begin to consider, judge and arrange life according to the holiness of God'. True repentance is a rebirth. By his forgiving grace God touches the depth of our conscience where the wound of sin cries out for healing. As the sinner turns to God with all his or her heart, God's powerful action of forgiveness grants them wholeness and integrity again.

A Presbyterian lady came to me for healing prayer on one occasion. She had cancer. Before we began to pray she said to me 'I know that I must now cleanse my heart from all sin, I must confess all my sins to God and receive his pardon'. She made a very moving and complete confession to the Lord. 'Now,' she said 'I am ready to receive healing prayer.'

Unconfessed sin will always block the peace of Christ. We cannot simultaneously seek peace from the Lord and at the same time hold on to the very thing which has robbed us of peace. A lady once rang me and asked me to pray for the healing of memories for a man with whom she had sexual relations. They had a bad disagreement and he did not want to see her again. It turned out that she was a married woman! When I said to her that the only healing for adultery was repentance and confession she became most irate.

The good news, of course, is that God delights in forgiving our sin and taking away our guilt. Unconfessed sin will always cause inner distress and block the flow of peace. This is how Scripture graphically describes the conflict:

> All the time I kept silent, my bones were
> wasting away
> with groans, day in, day out;
> day and night your hand
> lay heavy on me;
> my heart grew parched as stubble
> in summer drought.
>
> At last I admitted to you I had sinned;
> no longer concealing my guilt,
> I said, 'I will go to Yahweh
> and confess my guilt.
> And you, you have forgiven the wrong I did,
> have pardoned my sin'.
>
> Ps 32.3–5

God meets our confession and repentance with the gift of

total forgiveness. Clinging to unrepented or unconfessed sin blocks the experience of God's healing love.

When inner healing is being blocked through lack of repentance the person should always be encouraged to bring his sin confidently to the Lord in the sacrament of confession or according to his or her own denominational practice. Sometimes, sadly, the sin remains unconfessed because the person had a very bad experience of confession. If that is the case one should pray for the healing of that bad memory before encouraging the person to confess. The person should be asked to really forgive the confessor and to put his or her trust again in the sacraments of Christ.

Unforgiveness

Unforgiveness is a major block to inner healing. Just as openness to God, in love and contrition, is the prerequisite for the grace of repentance, so openness to one's neighbour, in acceptance and acknowledgement, is the prerequisite of the grace of forgiveness. If a person seeking the healing of relationships continues to experience resentment and bitterness the block may be an unforgiving heart.

'I will forgive, but I will never forget' is not a Christian approach to forgiveness. Forgiveness brings with it a total acceptance of the other person. We no longer see the person with the eyes of the sinned against; rather, we see the person with the eyes of a sinner who has also been forgiven.

Gordon Wilson of Enniskillen gave the whole world a perfect example of Christian forgiveness. He was standing with his daughter at the Remembrance Day parade in Enniskillen in 1987 when a massive IRA bomb exploded without warning and killed eleven people. Among the dead was his daughter Marie. He spoke on prime-time television (I saw

him on CNN news in San Francisco) about the great loss
he and his wife had sustained. Then he thrilled millions
around the world by saying that he and his wife had forgiven
the bombers and that they prayed each night for them. The
world would have understood if Mr Wilson had proclaimed
his undying hatred for the bombers. Some, indeed were
disappointed that he did not do so. But this devout Method-
ist knew his Lord and he knew that our Lord, who forgave
his own executioners, gives to each of us that same power
to forgive. There are no half-measures in Christian forgiveness. There are no unforgivable people in a Christian's
world.

The blockage in inner healing may be a half-hearted
assent towards forgiveness. I once had a frustrating experience trying to help a very hurt woman. Each time she
would go through the motions of forgiveness. I thought
she had forgiven. But the resentments came back. Then I
began to realize that instead of really forgiving she was
simply trying to find good excuses. When she found what
she thought was a good excuse she would forgive. The next
day, however, the excuse did not seem all that good and
her resentments returned. In the end I had to recognize
that she was not prepared to offer true Christian forgiveness
in the sense in which C. S. Lewis describes it:

Real forgiveness means looking steadily at the sin, the
sin that is left over without any excuse, after all allow-
ances have been made, and seeing it in all its horror,
dirt, meanness and malice, and nevertheless being wholly
reconciled to the man who has done it. That and only
that is forgiveness.[4]

Before any inner healing could bind up her wound this

woman had to pray for the grace of fundamental conversion.

The personality that has been warped by hurts and unforgiveness can only enter into peace by welcoming the gift of
metanoia, of that radical conversion which brings with it a
're-orientation of the personality'. Faced with the impasse
of unforgiveness in the heart of a hurt person we should
encourage them to listen to the words of Jesus, 'Father,
forgive them for they don't know what they are doing', and
we should ask them to pray for that same grace. We should
encourage the person with the assurance that he must be
patient with himself and ask for the gift of the Holy Spirit.

Guilt

When we do wrong we experience 'guilt feelings'. The
reason for these feelings is that we recognize that we have
acted in a way which is contrary to our sense of what is
right and good. If we had no reason, no conscience, we
would never experience 'guilt feelings'. The frightening
thing about the psychopath is that he can commit terrible
evil, like murder, without ever feeling guilty.

Feeling guilty, then, is the appropriate way to feel when
we sin. In sinning we violate not just some moral law but
also our own conscience, our own sanctuary. The Second
Vatican Council tells us that 'conscience is man's worst
secret core, and his sanctuary. There he is alone with God
whose voice echoes in his depths'.[5] It is in our conscience
that we become aware of God's law. The Council said:

Deep within his conscience man discovers a law which
he has not laid upon himself but which he must obey. Its
voice, ever calling him to love and do what is good and

avoid evil, tells him inwardly at the right moment: do this, shun that. For man has in his heart a law inscribed by God. His dignity lies in observing this law, and by it he will be judged.[6]

When we act against our conscience we feel guilty. That is a sign of a healthy conscience. Indeed it is the grace and light of the Holy Spirit inviting us to turn again to God and seek forgiveness.

When we acknowledge and confess our sin and ask God's pardon, God takes away our sin. Normally too we are freed from all feelings of guilt and know instead the renewed peace of the Lord. While feelings of guilt and shame are the direct consequence of sinful behaviour, feelings of peace and joy are the direct consequence of having our sins forgiven. Once our sins have been forgiven, feelings of guilt would no longer be appropriate. Such feelings, instead of calling us to conversion, would be enticing us to doubt or even deny the forgiveness which we have received.

We can speak, then, of good guilt and bad guilt. Good guilt is the appropriate response to sin; bad guilt is the inappropriate response to forgiveness. The appropriate response to forgiveness is praise and thanksgiving. 'Go in peace, your sins are forgiven'. The inability to give praise and thanks may be a sign of bad guilt.

Bad guilt blocks inner healing. The person continues to feel guilty even though God has forgiven his or her sins. The bad guilt must be addressed in prayer. I find the most effective prayer for dealing with bad guilt is the Eucharist. In the second eucharistic prayer we pray, after the Consecration, 'We thank you for counting us worthy to stand in your presence and serve you'. I ask the person to hear these words deeply, and every time he or she comes into God's presence let that be the first prayer. Every time he or she is attacked with the bad guilt the immediate response should be 'I thank you for the wonder of myself' and 'I thank you that you count me worthy to stand in your presence and serve you'.

Locked into bad guilt we often find a sense of shame. The person is ashamed not of some bad action in the past but of himself. He may be a shamed person. Our society uses shame to control people. The mother may say to the little child, 'Don't do that, shame on you'; the teacher may say to the young boy, 'Your older brother would never do that, shame on you'; an irate parent may say to the adult son or daughter 'You ought to be ashamed of yourself'. Bad guilt, compounded by shame, presents a formidable obstacle to inner healing. With such a person we have to start with the basics, namely the healing of the self-image. We have to teach the person to live by the creative Word of God, which assures him that he is 'precious in God's sight' and not by the destructive word, which accuses him of being an object of shame.

We should introduce the person suffering from this bad guilt to St Bernard's approach:

What I can't obtain by myself, I appropriate to myself with confidence from the pierced side of the Lord because he is full of mercy. The mercy of God is, therefore, my merit. And what about my righteousness? O Lord, I shall remember only your righteousness. It is also mine because you are God's righteousness for me.

If none of the four barriers mentioned in this chapter is present, or if all barriers have been resolved, and yet the person is not receiving peace through inner healing prayer,

we may then have to consider the presence of the fifth
barrier. This is a bondage of some kind, and will be
explored in Chapter 6.

6

Breaking the Bondage

In praying for inner healing we have the Word of God to guide us and the Spirit of God to empower our ministry. The Word of God has been called 'a light for my path and a lamp for my way'. With that light we can enlighten the inner world of the person. We have seen how the light of the words 'I thank you for the wonder of myself' lights up the whole dimension of self-acceptance. So, too, the words 'bless Yahweh my soul, all that is in me bless his holy name' light up everything that is going on in the memory bank. And the words 'forgive seventy times seven' enlighten the quality of relationships with those who have hurt us. We need this light in the ministry of inner healing.

It sometimes happens that someone, despite getting the 'all clear' in the areas of the four barriers discussed in the last chapter, is still not receiving the gift of peace. Then we have to discern, with the help of God, what is blocking the peace. If the person is open to the Spirit of God in his or her own spirit – open to accepting self gratefully, open in repentance and forgiveness – but is still not receiving peace, we have to discern whether there is some form of evil spirit, some demonic interference, with the person's freedom.

In the introduction to the New Rite of Penance we are told that 'discernment of spirits is indeed a deep knowledge of God's working in the human heart, a gift of the Spirit, and an effect of charity' (no 10). We believe that there are three spirits at work in the life of each human being, namely God's Spirit, the human spirit, and the evil spirit. We have to discern what comes from each of these spirits.

The Holy Spirit is the spirit of love, joy and peace; the spirit of truth and freedom; the spirit of counsel and fortitude; the spirit of encouragement and consolation. We discern his presence through his fruits. The evil spirit is the spirit of darkness and fear; it is 'the father of lies' and 'a murder from the beginning'; it is the 'unclean spirit', the 'accuser of the brethren' and the enemy of our human race. We can discern the evil spirit's presence also through its destructive fruits.

Sometimes the barrier to inner healing may be the action of the evil spirit. This does not necessarily imply that the person who is the victim of the evil spirit's action is bad or evil. It may mean simply that while the person was very hurt or weak the evil spirit took advantage and used the hurt or weakness to form a bondage.

The story of two mothers, both suffering from the shock of murder in their families, will illustrate this. While on a parish mission in the west of Scotland a lady came to see me during a house Mass. Everyone at the Mass was coming to confession. She came in and said, 'I can't go to confession, but I would like to talk'. I presumed that she could not come to confession because she may have been married outside the Church. 'Oh no', she said, 'I can't forgive, so there is no point in me going to confession'.

She then told me her sad story. Her only son was serving a life sentence for the murder of a young man. She was

convinced that this young man and his family goaded her
son beyond endurance and that he had no intention of
killing. But he was found guilty and sentenced. Now her
heart was full of hatred. 'I have no peace', she said, 'because
I hate them and I can't forgive them'. I asked her 'Would
you like to be able to forgive them?' She responded immediately 'I would love to. It is like a cold stone in my heart'.

She was a good woman, a devout Catholic. I saw her at
all the services of the mission. I had not realized until then
she was not coming to the sacraments. Here was a very
clear case of a woman deeply desiring to do the Christlike
thing and forgive and not being able to do it. Through the
tragic killing on her son's part she now found herself
bonded through hatred with the family whose son he killed.
She was in real bondage. She was not free.

I explained to her that Jesus would set her free and give
her the power to forgive. As I was praying with her I bound
that evil spirit of hatred in the name of Jesus and silently
commanded it to depart and never return. I then asked the
Lord to fill her with his forgiving love. The hatred and
coldness in her heart immediately left her and she knew
she had forgiven them. During that house Mass she came
to the sacraments for the first time in years with great joy.

Almost exactly the same situation confronted me some
time later in the east of Scotland. I was conducting a
renewal day in a parish. A lady came to see me and with
her beautiful sad voice she said, 'I have just come in for a
chat because I can't go to confession'. Again I thought she
may have been married outside the church. 'No', she said,
'my son was murdered in London and since then I can't
come to the sacraments because I hate his murderer and
his mother. If I can't forgive there is no point in me going
to the sacraments, is there?' When I asked her whether she

would like to be able to forgive I got the very same answer. 'I would love to. It's like a cold stone in my heart'.

I explained to her that Jesus would take away the stone and enable her to forgive. 'I hope to God he will', she said, 'because I am demented.' I used exactly the same silent prayer, binding the evil spirit in Jesus' name and commanding it to depart. I asked the Lord to fill her with the Holy Spirit and with his forgiving love. She was instantly set free. Later on that day she came up during the healing service for the anointing. She was full of joy and said, 'I have forgiven him and I have forgiven his mother and I am praying for them'.

She was a good woman but through the murder of her son she was bonded in hatred to the man who killed him and also to his mother. She had lost her freedom in relation to them. She was in bondage to them. This bondage robbed her of the very means of peace. She could not forgive. In both this and the former case the bondage had to be broken before they came into the freedom of forgiveness.

I use this image to help myself think about what is actually happening in these cases. Suppose you are washing the dishes in the sink and you cut your finger on a broken glass. You immediately rinse the finger under the tap, put on some TCP and a plaster. Your finger will be fine in the morning. But suppose you cut your finger on a rusty nail and carry on doing what you are doing all day. By evening there is a throb in the finger and then you wash it and put a plaster on. How will the finger be in the morning? It will have festered. Before the finger heals you have to get the poison out. For the healing of the nice, clean cut all you need is the TCP and the plaster; for the healing of the festered finger you have to get the poison out first.

Sometimes, I think, a similar thing happens in the

spiritual world. If a person has been hurt badly, but the wound remains clean and uninfected, inner healing is all that is needed. But if the evil spirit infects the wound with its poison of bondage, inner healing will not work. First the bondage must be broken.

We call this ministry of breaking the bondage 'the deliverance ministry'. The deliverance ministry is based on a number of truths which not all Christians accept. As I mentioned in the first chapter there are some theologians and Scripture scholars who simply deny both the reality of evil spirits and the consequent need for any ministry of deliverance. As I wrote, 'biblical theories have pastoral implications. Demythologizing the New Testament teaching on the reality of evil spirits declares the ministry of exorcism, in all its forms, obsolete. But the discernment of the need for exorcism belongs to pastors and ministers rather than to academics and theologians'.

Had I approached my ministry to the two women mentioned above with the conviction that there are no evil spirits and consequently there can never be a need for deliverance, they would have remained in the bondage of hatred and unforgiveness. I would have tried to comfort, console and counsel them. But they had received all that from their parish community. And still they were bound in hatred.

I understand why many priests and ministers today never use this ministry. For the first ten years of my ministry I never saw any need for it. When people came with problems I would listen to them, counsel them to the best of my ability, hear their confession if they wished to confess and send them off with a word of encouragement.

I remained very much on the level of counselling. I celebrated the sacraments of anointing and reconciliation for sick and hurting people. Outside the sacramental context, however, I had no prayer ministry for them. I never prayed with them for inner healing. When I was going through the seminary I never heard of a ministry of inner healing. Similarly, I never saw the need for deliverance because I had forgotten altogether about the reality of evil spirits. I looked exclusively for psychological explanations; outside the sacramental celebrations I applied only counselling skills.

On 24 September 1975, during the first three-month renewal course at Hawkstone Hall, where I was director, I went to confession to a visiting priest, Fr Wilfrid Brieven, who was, at the time, secretary to Cardinal Suenens. Fr Brieven not only heard my confession but he prayed over me for a very long time. A deep peace settled on me and I knew that I was making a completely new commitment of my life to Christ. I also knew that my whole approach to priestly ministry would have to change. I was experiencing help in an altogether new way, not through the counselling skills of an expert but through the faith of a priest.

Describing the effects of this spiritual event in my own life I wrote three years later:

The way Fr Brieven prayed with me in celebrating the sacrament of reconciliation became the norm of my own celebration. And I saw marvellous results. As I prayed with people for inner healing I saw them being freed from deep resentments and anger, from bitterness and jealousy, from all kinds of things which had been robbing them of joy in the Lord. In the sacrament of reconciliation I saw the difference between the simple absolution with a few words of encouragement and the extended prayer for inner healing.[1]

I found my whole ministry of listening and counselling transformed through a prayer ministry for inner healing. On many occasions the prayer did not work. That always puzzled me. Why does a prayer for inner healing, which brings such peace to one person, fail to bring the same peace to another, even though the other seems to have exactly the same hurt and the same desire to be freed? I gradually became aware of the barriers to inner healing which I discussed in the last chapter. But I also became aware that besides barriers of a psychological or moral nature there could be barriers of a demonic nature. I had recovered my faith in the Church's teaching on the reality of evil spirits. I became aware that in some cases where the people failed to receive inner healing the real barrier was in some mysterious way outside themselves.

My first experience of the deliverance ministry was while I was trying to help a young married woman. She was married to a long-distance lorry driver. He had to drive all over Europe, sometimes as far as Rome. He would be away from home for days on end. She had become very suspicious that every time he went abroad he was being unfaithful to her. When she came to see me she was almost demented with these suspicions. She explained that he was a good, a loving and kind husband and that he would feel awful if he ever knew that she had such suspicions. At the same time she could not get them out of her mind. As I prayed with her I became aware that this suspicion was an evil thing, attacking her peace and threatening to undermine and destroy her marriage. I found myself saying, 'I bind this suspicion in the name of Jesus Christ and I command you evil spirit leave this daughter of God the Father and never return'. The prayer was said in silence. Then I prayed aloud for the Lord to bless her marriage and to fill her home with his Holy Spirit. She experienced a great peace and complete release from the suspicion. She began to send all her married women friends to see me. They came with the same request, 'I believe you have a great blessing for married couples'. She had told them about her release from her terrible suspicion and how God had blessed her marriage. She taught me how to speak about the ministry of deliverance. It is a great blessing.

As I reflected on that pastoral experience it became obvious to me that I would have wasted my time if I had tried to bring her to peace simply by counselling. She knew that the suspicion was irrational. She could give me all the good reasons why her husband would not be unfaithful. Yet she was, in her own words, 'demented'. I was deeply impressed myself at what had happened. Nothing in my theological formation had trained me to do what I had just done. I realized that I had performed some form of exorcism or deliverance and that some kind of evil spirit had departed. I had taught moral and pastoral theology to students for the priesthood for six years and I had never even mentioned a ministry of deliverance or exorcism. Looking back on those years I have to say that although I never formally gave up belief in the Church's teaching on evil spirits, my faith was totally inactive. I was aware that possession by the devil could take place in rare cases; I was also aware that if that happened the bishop would appoint a holy, wise and ascetical priest to deal with it. It would be no concern of mine.

I realized that throughout the Catholic Church, in most, if not in all the seminaries where priests were being trained, there would be no teaching on this ministry. That is why I said that I understand why so many priests and ministers do not use this ministry. Like myself, nobody taught them about it. The more I became aware of the need for this ministry, however, and the more I saw suffering people being set free, the more concerned I became to locate this ministry within my own Catholic tradition. It was an Anglican priest, Christopher Neil-Smith, who taught me how to do this. In 1977 Christopher, the official exorcist for the diocese of London, conducted a workshop on exorcism for a group of Catholics at Hawkstone Hall. He has a most blessed ministry of deliverance and has helped hundreds of people into freedom in the Lord. He began by saying that he was delighted and surprised to be addressing a group of Catholic priests, religious and laity on the subject of exorcism because he had learned most of what he knew from Catholic sources. This remark forced me to go back to the sources. I went back to the Church's tradition, to the manuals of moral theology which had been used in Catholic seminaries for centuries, and, to my great delight and relief, I discovered that what Christopher Neil-Smith said was true. Confessors throughout the centuries had been encouraged to use a silent prayer of simple exorcism to set people free.[2]

The Prayer for Deliverance

The prayer for deliverance is not an appeal to Jesus to drive away the evil spirit. It is a command, in the name of Jesus, directed to the evil spirit. This command is normally given in silence. The fact that, as a result of this silent command, a troubled person is set free is a clear sign that an intelligent being heard the command and obeyed.

Once we become aware that there is need for deliverance we should focus all our attention on the Lord. We do not focus on the evil spirit. The following steps can be helpful:

1   A prayer of praise. Devote a little time to rejoicing in Christ's great victory over Satan and evil;

2   Pray for Christ's protection on everyone involved. Christ is present to defend us and therefore we should have no fear of the evil one. We pray, 'Lord we claim your victory now. You are our protector and our deliverer';

3   A prayer of binding. Before we command the evil spirit to depart we bind it in the name of Jesus. For instance, 'I bind in the name of Jesus Christ every evil spirit'. If we have discerned that there is a spirit of fear or a spirit of unforgiveness it would be appropriate to say 'I bind you, spirit of fear, or spirit or unforgiveness, in the name of Jesus Christ.'

4   The direct command to the evil spirit to depart. 'I command you in the name of Jesus Christ, unclean spirit, to depart from this beloved son or daughter of the heavenly Father and never return. I command you to go to Jesus'. We let the Lord himself send the evil spirit to where it belongs. It is important to keep praising the Lord while commanding the evil spirit to depart. For instance, if there is a spirit of fear present you could be praising the Lord audibly and silently commanding the evil spirit to depart. When the person begins to join in the praise of God that is a good indication that something is happening and that the spirit has left. If the person cannot join in the praise he or she is still bound in some way. At that stage it is often helpful to ask the person what is going on inside and how he or she is feeling. We keep praising until the person feels free to join in.

5   Invoke the Holy Spirit to come and fill the person afresh. Where there was darkness we pray for the

Spirit of light; where there was fear we pray for the Spirit of courage; where there was sin we pray for the Spirit of holiness. Since the person has been chosen to be 'the temple of the Holy Spirit' we should invoke the Spirit with great confidence. The Spirit comes to reclaim, sanctify and fortify what rightly belongs to him.

We should never tell the person that we are going to pray for deliverance. It is sufficient to say, 'Let us bring this problem, this inner wound, this bondage to the Lord and ask for his blessing.' We silently command the evil spirit to depart. I believe the principle reason for this way of proceeding is this: we can never be a hundred percent certain that we are dealing with an evil spirit. If there is no evil spirit present the deliverance is not necessary. But, if the person has been told that he needs a deliverance, and then nothing happens, he or she would be left feeling that the evil spirit was still there. That is why we must always follow the prudential rule of silent prayer and refrain from indicating, in any way, that an evil spirit is at work in the person.

Sometimes it will be very important to have a follow-up ministry to the person. We should direct them to a good faith-sharing group or prayer group where possible and encourage the person to become actively involved in his or her local Christian community. The lack of a warm, welcoming community, where people know how to pray with one another, and know how to build one another up in the faith, is an incalculable impoverishment of Christian ministry today. With so many men and women, all endowed with the Holy Spirit, many of whom are already gifted and experienced in this ministry in the Spirit, there is no excuse

for people to have to go without the appropriate Christian
ministry.

7

Inner Healing and the Sacraments of Reconciliation and Eucharist[1]

Catholics automatically think of the barriers to inner healing in the context of the sacraments: they would see forgiveness, repentance freeing from guilt as the specific grace of the sacrament of reconciliation.

On Easter Sunday evening the risen Lord said to his disciples, 'Receive the Holy Spirit. For those whose sins you forgive, they are forgiven; for those whose sins you retain, they are retained' (Jn 20. 22). The Church's faith crystallized into the firm belief that that Easter gift of the risen Lord, namely the power to forgive sins through the Holy Spirit, remains with the Church. It remains specifically in the sacrament of reconciliation. When someone asked the great G.K. Chesterton why he became a Catholic he said simply 'because I wanted someone to use the power Jesus gave to the Church and say to me your sins are forgiven'. The desire to hear the forgiveness of God proclaimed through the power of the Holy Spirit is one of the deepest desires of the sinful heart.

Throughout the history of the Catholic Church there has been a great emphasis on confession and the forgiveness of sin. The practice of 'going to confession' was one of the distinctive hallmarks of Catholics. The experience of the Church throughout the centuries has been that a good confession brings great peace to the soul. Fr Bernard Häring describes peace. 'The biblical concept of peace is amazingly comprehensive. It includes salvation, wholeness, integrity, healthy and healing interpersonal relationships, cultural, economic and social relationships and transformations which serve the cause of peace and of wholeness and integrity'.[1]

God's gift of peace is lost through serious sin. If we knowingly and willingly do what is contrary to God's will our soul is bereft of peace. Only God's gift of forgiveness, in response to our contrite confession, restores our peace. While the peace of soul is lost through serious sin, our peace can be disturbed by what the New Rite of Penance calls 'the wound of sin'.

Wound of Sin

In the introduction to the New Rite of Penance we read: 'Just as the wounds of sin are varied and multiple in the life of individuals and of the community, so too the healing which penance provides is varied'.

We recognize two effects of sin: sin as an offence against God, causing an alienation between God and self; and the wound of sin, that is the inner hurt caused in a person by the sinful action or words. The sin itself will be manifested in a cold, deliberate malicious act of one kind or another; the wound of sin will reveal itself through some kind of re-action. Just as a person in pain may cry out, so a person with the wound of sin may very well 'strike out'.

For the sin itself we need God's forgiveness; for the

wound of sin we need the Lord's healing. Both are signified in the words of Absolution: 'Through the ministry of the Church may God give you pardon and peace'. Pardon is for the sin; peace is for the wound of sin.

New Emphasis

This is a new emphasis in our understanding of the sacrament of reconciliation. We always saw the sacrament as the great means of forgiveness. We did not, however, always focus on the healing power of the sacrament. We had lost sight of what the New Rite of Penance calls 'the wound of sin'.

If a husband and wife, for instance, have a nasty row, and they do not take time to show each other loving forgiveness, the hurts which they have inflicted on one another will remain unhealed. Very little provocation will be needed to spark off the next row. If they continue in this cycle of fighting, without really healing the wounds through loving and tender forgiveness, they will reach a stage in their relationship where the slightest thing will provoke a row. They will not be able to communicate with each other; they will blame one another; they will no longer be able to trust one another. The breakdown in their relationship will be caused by the inner wounds which they have inflicted on each other and which have been allowed to fester. They may even be blaming each other for the lack of communication or trust, whereas the real cause will be the unhealed wounds.

If they bring their wounds to the sacrament of reconciliation they will experience healing. They will be able peacefully to face the task of rebuilding their relationship. While the wounds remain unhealed this task will be impossible for them. Even if only one of them seeks healing for the wound of sin the total relationship will be transformed. The healed partner will no longer be re-acting out the inner wound, but responding in love.

Barbara tells the story of how God healed her marriage. She was praying for God to do something about her husband. He had no faith and was re-acting negatively to her strong faith. As she was asking God to change him for the better God let her see that he was not pleased with her prayer. She was sitting in judgement on her husband. The Lord taught her to pray this prayer: 'Lord, heal my marriage, but begin with me'.

She kept praying this prayer faithfully. She began to notice that her husband was going out on the same evening each week. He never said where he was going. On his return one evening he took her completely by surprise and announced that he was about to be received into the Church. His mysterious weekly trips were for instruction in the faith. From the moment she began to take responsibility for their relationship and ask God to begin the healing of their marriage in her, their relationship improved. The whole relationship changed because she was willing to ask the Lord to heal the wounds in herself.

The sacrament of reconciliation is for the healing of all inner wounds. When a Catholic speaks to me about a painful or broken relationship I always suggest that we should bring the relationship to the celebration of the sacrament and seek reconciliation. In the celebration we listen to the Word of God; we pray for discernment; we enter into deeper sorrow for sin; we confess our sins; we receive God's forgiveness for our sins and healing for the wounds of sins; in our purpose of amendment we promise God to do our best to avoid these sins and the occasion of sin in the future.

As the person seeks reconciliation with God in the sacrament he or she can be led to seek reconciliation with the person who has caused hurt and offence. The confessor leads the person in forgiveness prayer.

Role of Confessor

The New Rite of Reconciliation describes the confessor's role in this way:

> By receiving repentant sinners and leading them to the light of the truth, the confessor fulfils a paternal function: he reveals the heart of the Father and shows the image of Christ the Good Shepherd. He should keep in mind that he has been entrusted with the ministry of Christ, who mercifully accomplished the saving work of human redemption and by mercy and by his power is present in the sacrament (no 10).

The penitent should experience in the way in which the confessor receives him or her, 'the heart of the Father'. The confessor's role is to mirror the love and compassion of God. The penitent may arrive broken hearted, feeling cut off from God and full of confusion, shame and distress. In the confessor, the penitent should meet understanding, total acceptance, and great encouragement. The confessor has to reflect to the penitent the very acceptance of God the Father and the forgiving love of Christ.

The specific gift of confession is this: a person can bring to the sacrament all sins, no matter how serious, for which he is sorry; he can confess them with the certainty that God forgives the sins and heals the wounds of sin; and he has the assurance that confidentiality is guaranteed. In the

strictest sense the person can come to the sacrament and
unburden himself.

One lady who shed her burden described what happened
in this way:

It isn't easy to confess sins of a sexual nature, and it isn't
easy to break a long established habit. I had a strong
habit of masturbation which bothered me for many years.
You prayed over me and I felt a great weight being lifted
off me and a tremendous feeling of joy welling up within
me. I knew I had been set free. What I could not achieve
by my own efforts and good resolutions over the years
had happened instantaneously by the power of the Holy
Spirit made effective through your prayer. I will celebrate
forever the joy of that moment.

God's answer to sinfulness is forgiveness, healing and liber-
ation. Too often the human response is one of rationaliz-
ation. We psychologize away the sin. This lady had a strong,
compulsive habit. Some would say to her 'don't worry, this
can't be sinful. You haven't the freedom to commit sin'.
Such an approach takes the whole problem out of the
Lord's hands and leaves the penitent a victim to his or her
compulsion.

Instead of trying to rationalize away the sin we encourage
the penitent to be open to the presence of the Holy Spirit
for the full forgiveness of sin. As we say in the words of
Absolution, 'God the Father of mercies, through the death
and Resurrection of Jesus Christ, you have reconciled the
whole world to yourself and you have sent the Holy Spirit
among us for the forgiveness of sins'. The heart of the
sacrament is this new, forgiving, sanctifying and healing
presence of the Holy Spirit; Christ's Easter gift of the Spirit

is for the forgiveness of our sins. It is also our divine phys-
ician's remedy for the wounds of sin. The sacrament, celebrated with contrition for sin, truly 'binds up the broken
heart'.

The Eucharist and Inner Healing

We celebrate the Eucharist 'for the glory of God'. St Irenaus
told us that the 'glory of God is the human person fully
alive'. This means that when God is being glorified something is happening in us. We are being changed. Everything
in us which is in any way opposed to being fully alive in
the Spirit is being dealt with. If it is a sin, it is being
forgiven; if it is a wound of sin, it is being healed; if it is a
bondage of sin or evil, we are being set free.

The Second Vatican Council reminded us that the
Eucharist is the very centre of our worship of God and our
life as a people of God:

> The other sacraments, as well as every ministry of the
> Church and every work of the apostolate, are linked with
> the Holy Eucharist and are directed toward it. For the
> most blessed Eucharist contains the Church's entire spiri-
> tual wealth, that is, Christ Himself, our Passover and
> living bread. Through His very flesh, made vital and vital-
> izing by the Holy Spirit, He offers life to men. They are
> thereby invited and led to offer themselves, their labours,
> and all created things together with Him. Hence the
> Eucharist shows itself to be the source and the apex of
> the whole work of preaching the Gospel.[2]

In the celebration of the Mass we have 'the Church's
entire spiritual wealth'. Everything that Christ has done for

us is present in the mystery of the Mass. As the Vatican
Council says,

> At the Last Supper, on the night when He was betrayed,
> our Saviour instituted the Eucharistic Sacrifice of His
> Body and Blood. He did this in order to perpetuate the
> sacrifice of the Cross throughout the centuries until He
> should come again, and so to entrust to His beloved
> spouse, the Church, a memorial of His death and resur-
> rection; a sacrament of love, a sign of unity, a bond of
> charity, a pashcal banquet in which Christ is consumed,
> the mind is filled with grace, and a pledge of future glory
> is given to us.[3]

We participate in the mystery of the Eucharist by engaging
in four very familiar activities: we listen, we respond, we
offer, we receive.

We listen   We listen to the life-giving Word of God in the
first part of the Mass, the part we call 'the liturgy of
the Word'. We should listen with that hunger of Jeremiah:
'When your words came I devoured them' (Jer 15.16). The
Mass is a privileged moment for hearing the Word of God.

People sometimes complain that the Mass is boring. After
years of trying to think how to make the Mass 'more
interesting', it dawned on me that for many people the
Mass is boring because they do not listen to the Word of
God. The person who does not listen to the proclamation
of the Word of God during the 'liturgy of the Word' will
never be able to enter into the mystery of the Mass.

The Second Vatican Council reminded us that in the
Eucharist the Church lays before us two tables, the table
of the Word of God and the table of the body of the Lord.

We must feast at both tables. Listening avidly to the Word
of God opens our mind and heart to the healing which the
Eucharist offers us: 'Say but the word and I shall be healed'.

We respond   Hearing the Word of God enables us to
respond to what God is saying to us. We have multiple
responses in the Mass: prayers for mercy and forgiveness;
hymns and prayers of praise and thanksgiving; prayers of
intercession and petition; times for silent adoration and
contemplation.

In the first part of the Mass we deal with a major barrier
to inner healing, namely unrepentance. We acknowledge
that we are sinners. We ask God's pardon. Putting our heart
into the responses deepens our faith and spiritually prepares
us for the sacrifice which we offer to God. As St Paul said,
'I urge you, then, brothers, remembering the mercies of
God, to offer your bodies as a living sacrifice, dedicated
and acceptable to God: that is the kind of worship for you,
as sensible people' (Rom 12.1).

We offer   The offering that we make of ourselves to God
is symbolized in the gifts we bring to the altar. We bring
gifts of bread and wine. These gifts represent ourselves,
represent 'all that is within us'. We offer to God not just
what is good and healthy, but what is sinful, weak and
wounded. In the Mass we should consciously offer to God
all our weaknesses: all our inner wounds and pain; all
resentment, anger and bitterness; all our broken promises
and sinful failures. Our gifts of bread and wine represent
all that.

A new relationship is created between the one who offers
the gift and the one who receives it. The one who offers
is the *giver*; the one who receives becomes the *thanksgiver*.

When you give a gift to a friend your gift represents yourself; it represents your love for your friend. By receiving your gift your friend reciprocates your love. He says, 'Yes, I am your friend and I am grateful to you for your gift of friendship'.

The same dynamic is at work when we give gifts to God. Our gift represents our love. By accepting our gift God reciprocates our love. God becomes *thanksgiver* to us for the gift we offer to him in the Mass. In God's grateful acceptance of the offering we are making of ourselves we have the answer to the first great barrier to inner healing, namely lack of self-acceptance. God's total acceptance of us in the Mass should become the norm of our self-acceptance. God accepts all those things about us which we may find it hard to accept: our sinfulness and weakness, our frustrations and disappointments. Everything within us, which could cause self-rejection, should be offered to God in the celebration of the Eucharist.

During our celebration of the Eucharist we have the most appropriate moment to act on Pope John Paul II's insight: 'He must with all his unrest, uncertainty and even his weakness and sinfulness, with his life and death, draw near to Christ. He must, so to speak, enter into him with his own self, he must "appropriate" and assimilate the whole reality of the Incarnation and the Redemption'.[4]

In the Eucharist we have the complete reality of the Incarnation and redemption present sacramentally on the altar. As we offer ourselves to God we open our whole lives to be filled with 'the utter fullness of God' (Eph 3. 19).

We receive Having offered our gifts, the symbol of ourselves, the priest prays, 'Let your Spirit come upon these gifts so that they may become for us the body and blood of Jesus Christ your Son'. The bread and wine, which represent us before God, through this wonderful action of the Holy Spirit, become for us the body and blood of the Lord. Our gifts have been accepted and transformed by God. We too have been accepted. There is, therefore, no place in our life for any false guilt. We can pray with confidence: 'We thank you for counting us worthy to stand in your presence and serve you'. The Mass deals with all bad guilt. Because God counts us worthy, we accept ourselves as worthy.

During Mass, too, we are invited to dismantle that other barrier to inner healing, namely unforgiveness. After the Consecration we invoke the Holy Spirit for the gift of unity: 'May all of us who share in the body and blood of Christ be brought together in unity by the Holy Spirit'. We surrender everything which is opposed to this unity in the Spirit: unforgiveness; condemnation and rash judgements; envy and jealousy; all lack of love.

In a symbolic gesture we manifest our unity. The priest says, 'Let us offer each other a sign of peace'. At this stage we generally offer our hand in peace and friendship to those around us. The sign of peace is extended not just to those who are physically close to us in the church. It is for those who are emotionally close to us, even though they may be many miles away. In the Eucharist we are in the right space to offer our full forgiveness to everyone in our life.

Having shared that sign of unity we are now ready to receive. We receive Holy Communion. Our very approach to the altar is a proclamation that we are at peace with our brothers and sisters. Holy Communion is not just an act of union between Christ and the individual; it is a declaration of our intention to live in unity with all. Holy Communion is a sacrament. As the Council put it: it is 'a sacrament of love, a sign of unity, a bond of charity'.[5] Holy Communion presupposes that I love and forgive my enemies; it assumes that I have confessed all grave sin and that I am sorry for all my sins; it implies that I am actively seeking unity and peace with everyone in my life.

The bread of life which we receive in Holy Communion is rich in the Lord's promise: 'I am the living bread which has come down from heaven. Anyone who eats this bread will live for ever; and the bread that I shall give is my flesh for the life of the world' (Jn 6.51). The 'living bread' which we receive in Holy Communion is for the life of the world. It is for that abundant life which the Lord came to give to each of us. Consequently, as we celebrate the Eucharist, as we feast on the 'living bread' of Christ's body we can say with great confidence 'say but the word and I shall be healed'.

8

Praying for Physical Healing

Praying for physical healing is much more straightforward than praying for inner healing. We see a person who is obviously sick, or in pain. We impose hands on the person and ask the Lord to heal. We can pray like that anywhere, at any time. 'But I don't have a gift of healing' some people may say. That may be true, but they do have a gift of prayer. We are talking not about healing so much as about *praying*. The ministry is not 'a healing ministry', it is a 'ministry of prayer for healing'. The ministry is not what we do through our own gifts, but what we do 'in the name of Jesus'. Jesus himself said, 'In my name . . . they will lay their hands on the sick, who will recover' (Mk 16.18).

Sacrament of Anointing

We have, of course, an official prayer for healing in the Church. St James wrote: 'If one of you is ill, he should send for the elders of the church, and they must anoint him with oil in the name of the Lord and pray over him. The prayer of faith will save the sick person and the Lord will raise him up again; and if he has committed any sins, he will be forgiven' (James 5.14). In the Catholic Church we recognize this anointing in the name of the Lord as 'the sacrament of the sick'.

A sacrament is a personal encounter with the risen Lord. We believe that Jesus meets the sick person in love and forgiveness and with the gift of 'life in abundance'. The Vatican Council tells us that, in this sacrament, priests 'by the Anointing of the sick relieve those who are ill'.[1] Through the vagaries of our history the sacrament of the sick became the 'last anointing', extreme unction. The sacrament was not administered to the sick person until he or she was in danger of death. While the sick person was still fighting for life, the sacrament was not celebrated. As a result, we have no tradition in the Church of preparing the sick for their anointing. In the not so distant past, indeed, it would have been almost impossible to sit down with a sick person and start preparing for the celebration of the anointing. That would have been perceived as a preparation for death. The relatives would have objected.

We have a very different perception of the purpose of the sacrament today. As the Council says, it is 'to relieve the sick', it is for their healing and wholeness. The Church proposes to us today very direct prayers for the healing of mind and body. The expectation in our hearts, as we celebrate the sacrament of anointing, must correspond to the prayers on our lips.

A religious sister once rang me and asked if she could bring a lady, Pamela, who was suffering from Multiple Sclerosis for anointing and prayer. They would have to make a journey of over 300 miles. I almost panicked. What if nothing happens? The poor woman, after such an effort and such a long journey, would be very disappointed! I realized that I was looking for an excuse to say no. Instead, thank God, I said yes.

I met this lady again, fourteen years after her visit. She told me that the Lord had completely healed her of MS. She kindly agreed to share her testimony with the readers of this book. She wrote to me on 3 March 1994 as follows:

I was first diagnosed as having MS (Multiple Sclerosis) in April 1975. That followed years of doubt and worry that perhaps there was nothing really wrong with me after all: despite a lot of trouble in walking and a lack of sensation in my legs. For a long time the doctors thought I was suffering from spinal disc problems – and, indeed, I had two operations for disc trouble, one in 1969 and the next in 1974. It was after the last one that it was realised that something else was amiss. By then I was also having 'bladder problems' which finally led to total incontinence. It was only then that I was tested for MS and the diagnosis confirmed.

During the years 1975–1978 I gradually became more disabled. I could only walk a short distance before pain would bring me to a halt; the lack of co-ordination in my legs spread to my hands, so I devised a way of teaching which required virtually no writing on the blackboard but used 'ready prepared' OHP transparencies; and the loss of feeling in my legs meant that I needed hand controls to drive a car. In the summer of 1978 I had a Urinary Diversion operation in order to cope with the bladder incontinence.

I think it was in January 1979 that my head called me to her office one day. She asked me if I would be prepared to drive her to Hawkstone Hall one day towards the end of February. . . . When she went on to explain to me that the reason for the trip was so that Fr Jim McManus could pray with me to be healed, I found

myself in a quandary. For the next few weeks I wondered,
'Help! How do I get out of this?' A surprising reaction I
suppose, but it made me take a good look at myself.
I found I was scared to be healed because I was unsure
of my identity without MS. I had gone beyond accepting
the disease as God's will for me to using it for my very
identity. It had become a crutch on which I depended so
much that I didn't know who I would be without it. I
suppose I lived for the acclaim people gave me for carrying on stoically; I used the disease to avoid doing what I
did not really like doing. I had shut God out and not
only accepted MS, but allowed it to become my god so
that my life was an 'ego trip' instead of a 'God trip'. Now
the question was posed: 'was I prepared to let go of
myself and let God in – even if that meant giving up the
identity I had built up for myself?'

Finally the day for the trip arrived. We left Glasgow
early one morning and drove to Hawkstone Hall, in my
hand-controlled car, in time for lunch. After lunch, Jim
led us to a small room. I cannot remember very much
about the surroundings – my mind was still in turmoil.
Although I knew I wanted whatever God wanted, I was
still somewhat apprehensive. All I remember clearly is
Jim saying he would use the prayers of the Anointing of
the Sick and anoint me. And that is simply what he did.

We were very soon on our way back to Glasgow.
Immediately I felt a deep sense of peace; gone was the
turmoil that had been with me since the visit was suggested. I experienced a feeling of tremendous energy and
happiness that lasted for weeks. I also vividly remember
the surprise at not feeling tired the next day from such a
journey. But it was the following Sunday that I was to
experience the full meaning of healing. I was in the bath

in the early evening and, for the first time in at least three years, I felt the water. Just to make sure, I turned on the hot tap again and felt the warmth of the water lap around my legs. You can imagine how I felt! I was singing and shouting for sheer joy. I wanted to share it with my friends, but there was no one at the other end of the telephone line! It was a precious moment God and I had together – and one I shall never forget. But the most important change that took place was the fact that I knew God loved me for who I was, not for anything I could do for him – but just because I was me.

It took me a year to persuade the doctors that I didn't need to waste time on hospital visits any more and a little longer to persuade the DHSS that I didn't require a Mobility Allowance and the DVLC that I could use my feet to drive normally.

Ten years later my Urologist had to reverse the diversion (as a result of a kidney problem which had developed in the past two years). He was convinced that I would be incontinent again, and offered me counselling to help come to terms with that condition. Imagine his surprise when he realised I was fully continent; as he remarked, even if it was simply a case of misdiagnosis, my bladder should not work after lying unused for ten years. He maintains that there is no doubt that there has been a 'Divine intervention'; as he put it, 'there is definitely no medical explanation'.

Pamela's testimony is full of enlightening observations. She had to struggle with the question Jesus asked the paralysed man at the Pool of Bethzatha: 'Do you want to be well again?' (Jn 5.6). In that struggle she realized that she had come to depend on her sickness. It was her crutch. Not only that, it was becoming the source of her identity, even her god. Pamela's reflections on her feelings bring out well the difference between disease and illness. While disease affects the body, illness affects the way the sick person copes. Pamela's illness meant that she was beginning to cope by depending on the MS, as 'her crutch'. Her friends admired her courage. She kept on being a very successful teacher. And she could use her sickness to avoid what she did not want to do.

While Pamela was trying to find a way out of coming for anointing and healing prayer, I was momentarily trying to find a way of stopping her from coming. The journey would be too much: if she didn't get a healing, after such a long and exhausting journey, she would be bitterly disappointed. Pamela describes the moment of ministry in this way: 'All I remember clearly is Jim saying he would use the prayers of the anointing of the Sick and anoint me. And that is simply what he did'. She makes it very clear that the healing came through the sacrament of anointing. Within the Rite of Anointing we have both the ministry of the word and the ministry of the anointing with prayer for healing. Let us remind ourselves of the various moments in the celebration:

1 The priest welcomes those who gather for the anointing and says, 'My dear friends, we are gathered here in the name of the Lord Jesus Christ who is present among us'. This gives the celebration its focus: Christ is present;

2 Having called everyone present to a deeper faith awareness of the presence of Christ, the priest then says, 'Let us therefore commend our sick brother/ sister to the grace and power of Christ, that he may save him/her and raise him/her up'.

Right at the beginning of our celebration, then, we commit the sick person to the power of Christ. In the case of Pamela, her friend and I would have very consciously and confidently placed her in Christ's hands.

3   We are then invited to prepare ourselves for 'this holy anointing' by acknowledging our own sinfulness and our need for God's gracious forgiveness. (The sick person has the opportunity to celebrate the sacrament of reconciliation at this moment also.);

4   The Word of God is then proclaimed from the Gospel or one of the other New Testament writings. This proclamation calls the sick person and those present to a renewed faith in the healing love and power of Christ;

5   The priest preaches a short homily or shares his faith in the sacrament after the proclamation of the Word. I normally simply remind the sick what the Church believes about this sacrament. In the introduction to the new Rite of Anointing we read: 'This sacrament gives the grace of the Holy Spirit to those who are sick: by this grace the whole person is helped and saved, sustained by trust in God, and strengthened against the temptations of the Evil One and against anxiety over death'. I would have pointed out to Pamela that she was about to receive from God a new gift of the Holy Spirit and I would have invited her to open her whole heart to welcome this gift;

6   Then all present begin to pray for the sick person. This time of prayer is concluded with the words 'Give life and health to our brother/sister on whom we lay our hands in your name'. The priest lays his hands

on the sick person's head and invites the family, or close friends, or other parish ministers to do likewise;

7   The priest then blesses the oil for the anointing. This prayer of blessing builds up the sick person's faith for the anointing: 'God of all consolation you chose and sent your Son to heal the world. Graciously listen to our prayer of faith: send the power of your Holy Spirit, the Consoler, into this precious oil, this sooth-ing ointment, this rich gift, this fruit of the earth. Bless this oil† and sanctify it for our use. Make this oil a remedy for all who are anointed with it; heal them in body, in soul, and in spirit, and deliver them from every affliction. We ask this through Our Lord Jesus Christ'. A powerful prayer of blessing in which the Church concentrates the mind and heart of all present on God's healing love;

8   After this preparation through the asking of pardon for sin, the renewal of faith through listening to the word of God, and the prayers of the community the sick person is then anointed with the words, 'Through this holy anointing may the Lord in his mercy and love help you with the grace of the Holy Spirit. May the Lord who frees you from sin save you and raise you up';

9   The priest leads those present in more prayer for healing. One of the prayers set out in the rite reads as follows: 'Lord Jesus Christ, our Redeemer, by the grace of your Holy Spirit cure the weakness of your servant. . . . Heal his/her sickness and forgive his/her sins; expel all afflictions of mind and body; mercifully restore her/him to full health, and enable him/her to resume his/her former duties, for you are Lord for ever and ever'.

The liturgical rite of the sacrament prepares the person for real openness to the Holy Spirit. All the elements of openness are there: the confession of our sins; the listening to the Word of God; the renewal of our faith in God's healing love; our willingness to receive a new gift of the Spirit. Whoever celebrates the sacrament with this openness always receives a great blessing. It may not always be the blessing of physical healing, but it will certainly be a blessing of inner healing. Pamela first became aware of her inner healing: 'I felt a deep sense of peace: gone was the turmoil that had been with me since the visit was first suggested'. And she identified inner healing as the greatest gift which she received: 'But the most important change that took place was the fact that I knew God loved me for who I was, not for anything I could do for me – but just because I was me'.

Not everyone, as we know, experiences physical healing through the anointing as Pamela did. A priest who reviewed my book, *The Healing Power of the Sacrament*, made the comment that I only mentioned the 'successes'. What about all the times when people did not experience healing? I presume he meant physical healing and I cannot answer this question. We do the asking, God does the healing. I would love to see every sick person healed. But God loves them infinitely more than I do. And God is with them in the sacrament.

When we are celebrating the sacrament of anointing we believe that Christ himself is present, blessing the sick person through our ministry and filling them afresh with the Holy Spirit. We ask Christ with total confidence to heal the sick person in body, mind and spirit. Then we leave the final result to him. We cannot say that in Pamela's

case the sacrament was a success but in John's case, because
he did not receive physical healing, it was a failure.

Jane, a paralysed woman, was preparing to go to Lourdes
with great faith. She was convinced that she would be
healed. A confrere of mine, who was her close friend, feared
that she would return very disappointed. On her return she
was still paralysed. My confrere said to her, 'Were you very
disappointed when you weren't cured?' 'Oh, no', she said,
'I received something much better. I received the grace to
accept myself just as I am. So, I am very happy.'

Healing means wholeness and wholeness is the effect
of spiritual well-being, not just physical well-being. If, for
instance, a selfish, arrogant, and mean man goes into hospital with a cancerous tumour and comes out a selfish,
arrogant and mean man, without a cancerous tumour,
the cancer was cured, but the person was not healed. On the
other hand, if he came out of hospital a loving, kind and
generous man, in a terminal condition, he would have been
healed although the cancer was not cured. Healing is what
happens in the whole person, not just in the diseased organ.
Jane was healed at Lourdes, healed through the grace of
self-acceptance.

Pamela's story has deepened within me the conviction
that we must give time to the celebration of the sacrament
of anointing. We must have a lively faith in its healing
purpose; we must involve as many of the family and friends
as possible in the celebration, urging them to pray with
faith; we must expect both inner and physical healing
through the sacrament; we must ensure through preaching,
teaching and witnessing, that the parish community is fully
aware of the great healing gift God has given to the Church
in this sacrament; the parish community must support the

celebration of this sacrament just as it supports the celebration of other sacraments.

How wonderful it would be if members of the parish visited the sick person in preparation for the anointing. They could pray with the sick person, share the Scriptures on the healing love of God, and witness to what Christ is doing through the anointing. In this way they would prepare the person to be more fully open to the healing grace of the sacrament. Then, having prepared the person for the sacrament they could join the priest in the celebration.

Other Ways of Praying with the Sick[2]

Praying for physical healing is not, of course, in any way limited to the sacrament of anointing. There are many different forms of praying for healing in the Church. We have para-liturgical healing services. We have 'healing teams' in prayer groups and in some parishes. There are pilgrimages to the shrines of Our Lady. Eucharistic ministers, as they bring Holy Communion to the sick and house-bound, pray for healing while a growing number of parishes celebrate 'a healing Mass' a few times a year. Some parishes have a parish celebration of the sacrament of anointing for the sick and the elderly; a growing number of people, whether they be priests, religious or laity, now pray spontaneously for any sick person they meet or who may ask for their prayer. Our faith in the healing ministry of Christ in the Church is clearly being restored.

Healing of Agoraphobia

During a parish mission the parish priest asked me to visit a house and pray with a lady called Claire who suffered severely from agoraphobia. She got a complete release from this terrible affliction. Claire describes her condition and healing in this testimony.

As far back as I can remember, I never had a lot of confidence. A year before my mother died in 1979, I had panic attacks while out shopping, taking the two children to school or even just in the street. Everything I took for granted and loved to do became a nightmare. In fact it was the start of years of Agoraphobia. This fear got so bad I stopped going out. Although sometimes I was able to go with my husband in his car, but always with panic and my heart beating out of my body. There were days when I couldn't go out at all. In fact these days turned into weeks and sometimes months, but the worst was when I started having attacks at home. I would be so frightened of panic attacks that somebody had to stay with me. Sometimes my husband would take me for a walk at night. I would put my hand on his arm and he would be soaking with perspiration from me. We would only walk 20 or a 100 yards at the most depending on how I felt.

In 1990 our parish priest, Father McGuire came over to see us. My husband was with me because I was having a bad time. He asked if he could bring over Father McManus the next day as they were having a Healing Service at the Church and it was impossible for me to go. The next day I waited for Father. I did not know what to expect as I had prayed for years. When Father came into the living room I thought – 'Oh my God, please, please help me'. Father McManus put his hands on my head. My husband and Father McGuire also laid hands on me. Father McManus started praying. I don't know what he said as I was crying so much, but I felt hope in me and also a sensation like an electric shock going through me, then a feeling of peace.

The Lord had set her free. She was able to live a normal life. As she said, 'I felt strength, peace and joy. I knew I was not alone, the Holy Spirit was guiding me'.

Three of us prayed with Claire, her husband, her parish priest and myself. And there was her own heartfelt appeal to the Lord: 'Oh my God, please, please help me'. I believe that the presence of her husband was all important for the prayer. He had suffered with her for years. He laid his hands on her with great faith and prayed. The Lord heard his prayer.

A lady who had suffered exactly as Claire, even more acutely, told me about a similar healing. She was hospitalized several times for her agoraphobia. She had panics both inside and outside the house. Her parish priest persuaded her to go and stand at the door of the Church during the parish mission healing service. She told me that she approached the door with great anxiety. Then something happened and she found herself in the body of the church. She joined the crowds on the way up for anointing with blessed oil. She received her blessing and never had another attack of panic. Months after this healing she told me that her greatest joy now was travelling on the London Underground. She could never go down the Underground before her healing.

The interesting thing about this healing is that it seems to have happened as she was standing apart from the congregation, outside the door of the church. Fear of a panic attack prevented her from joining her community as they prayed for healing. The faith of her own parish community seems to have enveloped her, drawn her into congregation and freed her from the prison of agoraphobia.

Suffering and Healing in the Christian Life

Healing inevitably raises the question of suffering. If we pray for healing, does this mean that suffering is an evil to be avoided? Pamela was suffering pain and privation when the Lord healed her of MS. Today, fifteen years after the healing she so graphically described in her testimony, she is again seriously ill. In the spring of last year, 1993, she was diagnosed as having cancer and her consultant told her she would not live out the year.

Her parish priest asked her, 'Spiritually are you diminished by such extensive suffering?' She responded,

No, on the contrary, I think I've grown a lot. Quite definitely I've learned a lot about myself and learned to accept a lot in myself that I would have preferred to have left hidden. One of the most powerful things that I have come to realise is to acknowledge and accept my emotions as they arise. Very often these have been feelings that I would rather not admit to having experienced – loneliness, isolation, fear, doubt, anger, depression, anxiety – they've all been present at one time or another.

She clearly identifies the source of her self-acceptance:

Another thing that has developed is my personal relationship with Christ – by telling him exactly how I feel and knowing that I am not only accepted with those feelings, even if they are negative, but loved and cherished for

simply being me. I now find Christ to be the closest
friend I have – he and I can share everything.[3]

Pamela has discovered what John Paul calls the 'Gospel
of suffering'. At first sight this phrase might seem a con-
tradiction in terms: how can there be a gospel, a 'good
news' of suffering? Our society abhors suffering. We want
to anaesthetize the whole world against it. We see suffering
as something to be avoided at all costs. How can the Pope
speak of 'a Gospel of suffering'?

In his encyclical on suffering, John Paul II clearly states
that suffering and death are evil, the ultimate consequence
of original sin. Christ came to deliver us from this evil. In
talking with Nicodemus Jesus said, 'Yes, God loved the
world so much that he gave his only Son, so that everyone
who believes in him may not be lost but may have eternal
life' (Jn 3.16). The ultimate evil would be the definitive
loss of eternal life. Pope John Paul writes, 'The only-begotten Son was given to humanity primarily to protect man
against this definitive evil and against *definitive suffering*'.[4]
Christ, in his redemptive work, struck, as the Pope says,
the 'transcendental roots of evil' which are grounded in sin
and death. 'He conquers sin by his obedience unto death,
and he overcomes death by his Resurrection.'[5]

For those who accept his salvation, Christ has destroyed
the *eternal* effects of sin, namely the loss of eternal life.
But the *temporal* effects of sin, namely, suffering and death,
remain in this world. The Pope writes:

Even though the victory over sin and death achieved by
Christ in his Cross and Resurrection does not abolish
temporal suffering from human life, nor free from suffering the whole historical dimension of human existence,

it nevertheless *throws a new light* upon this dimension and upon every suffering: the light of salvation.[6]

Christ enters into the world of suffering. He takes the suffering of the whole world upon himself. As the prophet foretold, 'a man of sorrows and familiar with suffering . . . and yet ours were the sufferings he bore, ours the sorrows he carried . . . he was pierced through for our faults, crushed for our sins. On him lies a punishment that brings us peace, and through his wounds we are healed' (Is 53.4–5). Christ entered into the very heart of our world of pain and suffering and by his own suffering and death broke the power of sin and death for each of us.

Because Christ is at the heart of all human suffering we can speak of a 'Gospel of suffering'. When I said to Pamela that I thought that only those who have found Christ in their suffering can really understand this kind of language, she replied, 'Absolutely! But there is no other language to describe what happens to you when you really accept Christ in your sickness and suffering. It is a gospel'. Pope John Paul writes: 'Down through the centuries and generations it has been seen that in suffering there is concealed a particular power that draws a person interiorly close to Christ, a special grace'.[7]

Suffering in itself is not a good thing. But a good thing is concealed in suffering, namely, 'a particular power that draws a person interiorly close to Christ'. When a person is united more intimately to Christ, through this special grace concealed in suffering, the whole nature of suffering is transformed. Indeed the person can then understand what St Paul meant when he wrote: 'It makes me happy to suffer for you, as I am suffering now, and in my own body to do what I can to make up all that has still to be undergone by Christ for the sake of his body, the Church' (Col 1.24).

Christ's redemption is infinite. We cannot add to it. 'But at the same time', Pope John Paul II writes,

> in the mystery of the Church as his Body, Christ has in a sense opened his own redemptive suffering to all human suffering. In so far as man becomes a sharer in Christ's suffering – in any part of the world and at any time in history – to that extent *he in his own way completes* the suffering through which Christ accomplished the Redemption of the world'.[8]

We can speak, therefore, of 'redemptive suffering'. Human suffering in and by itself has no redemptive value; we fight against suffering in every way we can. Human suffering, lovingly united to the suffering of Christ has a 'redemptive value'. Those who refuse to unite their suffering with Christ on the Cross can never recognize this value. It is a value which can be discerned only through the eyes of faith. It is a mystical value. That is why we should always pray for a renewal of faith for the sick person.

Without a renewed and a deepened faith the sick person may not be able to accept what the Church recommends in time of sickness: 'The Church exhorts them [the sick] to associate themselves willingly with the passion and death of Christ (see Romans 8.17), and thus contribute to the welfare of the people of God'. Indeed, the 'sustaining of trust in God' is considered one of the effects of the sacrament of anointing.[9]

Healing in the Spirit

As we approach our ministry to the sick we must be confident that we are bringing the sick into the loving presence of God. We entrust them to the God's loving care. This is the very best thing we can do for the sick. We pray confidently for healing, as Christ commands us. To some God grants restored health of mind and body; to others he grants inner healing and new freedom in the Spirit; while to others he grants the interior grace to unite their suffering with the suffering of Christ.

The Church has a message of great hope for the sick. There is multiple healing for body, mind and spirit, because there is healing in the Spirit.

Notes

Introduction

1 L'Osservatore Romano, 19 May 1986 (English edition).
2 The Mission of the Redeemer, 90.
3 General Audience, 30 November 1972.
4 Exhortation on Evangelisation, 75.
5 The Redeemer of Men, 8.
6 Exhortation on Evangelisation, 75.

1 Our Christian Vision of the World We Live In

1 Constitution on the Church in the Modern World, para 37.
2 Pope Paul VI, L'Osservatore Romano, 23 November 1972.
3 Encyclical on Holy Spirit, 29; cf. Constitution on the Church in the Modern World, 2.
4 Cit. Graham Twelftree, *Christ Triumphant: Exorcism Then and Now*, London 1985, 157.
5 C. S. Lewis, *The Screwtape Letters*, London 1944, 9.
6 L'Osservatore Romano, 23 November 1972.
7 Francis Wright Beare, *The Gospel according to Matthew*, Oxford 1981, 107.
8 John Richards, *But Deliver Us From Evil*, London 1974, 32.
9 Constitution on the Church in the Modern World, 37.
10 Dom Benedict Heron OSB, *Praying for Healing*, London 1989, 96.

2   Christ and the Spiritual World

1   R. Cantalamessa, *Jesus Christ the Holy One of God*, Slough 1991, 127.
2   Encyclical on Holy Spirit, 19.
3   L. Howard Marshall, *The Gospel of Luke*, Exeter 1978, 168.
4   George Montague, *Mark*, Ann Arbor 1981, 177.
5   James Dunn, *Jesus and the Spirit*, Philadelphia 1979, 48.
6   John P. Kealy, *Luke's Gospel Today*, New Jersey 1979, 286.
7   Encyclical on Holy Spirit, para. 21.

3   Jesus: Our Intercessor at the Right Hand of the Father

1   Constitution on the Church in the Modern World, 7.
2   Constitution on the Church in the Modern World, 40.
3   Decree on Ecumenism, 2.
4   Encyclical on Holy Spirit, 24.
5   Encyclical on Holy Spirit, 25.
6   Killian McDonnell and George Montague, *Christian Initiation and Baptism in the Holy Spirit*, Collegeville, 1991, 21.
7   St Thomas, Heb. cap. 8, lect. 2.
8   ST Thomas, in 2 Cor. cap. 3, lect. 2.
9   Cit. Edward O'Connor, *Pope Paul and the Holy Spirit*, Notre Dame, 1978, 154.
10   For these quotations from the Early Fathers and many more similar texts see the excellent history of the healing ministry, Norton Kelsey, *Healing and Christianity*, London 1973. For a very comprehensive study see the classical work by Evelyn Frost, *Christian Healing*, London 1940.
11   Ramsey MacMullan, *Christianizing the Roman Empire AD 100–400*, Yale, 1984, 41.
12   Ibid.
13   Constitution on the Church in the Modern World, 12.

4   Life in Abundance: Christ's Promise

1 Veritatis Splendor, 19.
2 Constitution on Divine Revelation, 10.
3 Veritatis Splendor, 85.
4 Constitution on the Church in the Modern World, 22.
5 Ibid.
6 The Redeemer of Man, 10.
7 Ibid.
8 Constitution of the Church in the Modern World, 9.
9 In 1973 I was asked by my Provincial to establish a centre
   for renewal in our stately mansion Hawkstone Hall, which
   had been for many years our seminary. Priests and religious
   Sisters and Brothers come from all over the world to our
   renewal courses. Each year there are three residential renewal
   courses. Each course lasts three months. Sixty-five partici-
   pants are accepted on each course. Since their inception
   these courses have been the source of great spiritual and
   personal renewal for thousands of religious men and women
   and priests. It was into this atmosphere of prayer and renewal
   that the priest in question walked.
10 Cit. Leanne Payne, *Restoring the Christian Soul through Heal-
    ing Prayer*, Eastbourne 1992, 31.
11 The Redeemer of Man, 10.
12 Constitution on the Church in the Modern World, 4.
13 C. S. Lewis, *Fern-Seed and Elephants*, Glasgow 1975, 40.
14 Confessions of St Patrick, 36.

5   Barriers to Inner Healing

1 The Redeemer of Man, 10.
2 New Rite of Penance, 6.
3 M. Maddocks, *The Christian Healing Ministry*, London 1985,
   p. 12.
4 C. S. Lewis, *Fern-seed and Elephants*, Glasgow 1975, 41.
5 Constitution on the Church in the Modern World, 16.
6 Ibid.

6 Breaking the Bondage

1 *Anointed with the Spirit*, NSC Publication, London 1978, 50.
2 St Alphonsus Liguori speaks for the Catholic tradition when
   he writes: 'Private exorcism is permissible to all Christians;
   solemn exorcism is permissible only to ministers who are
   appointed to it, and then only with the express permission
   of the bishop' (*Theologia Moralis*, III, 2, 492).

   The basic distinction is between simple and solemn exorcism. According to Noldin, the Jesuit manualist, simple
   exorcism is for the purpose of curbing the devil's power,
   while solemn exorcism is for the purpose of driving the devil
   out. Those who are possessed by the devil need solemn
   exorcism. This exorcism is reserved to the bishop. Noldin,
   however, encouraged confessors to use simple exorcism more
   frequently: 'It is much to be desired that ministers of the
   Church should perform simple exorcism more frequently,
   remembering the words of the Lord: In my name they shall
   cast out demons – this exorcism can be performed without
   the knowledge of the person' (*Theologia Moralis*, III, 59).

   Prummer, a Dominican manualist, said: 'Experience teaches that sometimes in the confessional, exorcism can be
   used secretly, without the penitent's knowledge' (*Theologia
   Moralis*, II, 365). In the same volume Prummer also wrote:
   'Nowhere is it forbidden to the laity to use private exorcism'.
   Marc, a Redemptorist manualist, wrote: 'Private exorcism is
   lawful to all, especially priests, nor is there any special permission of the bishop required' (*Institutiones Morales Alphonsi-
   ane* I, 622).

   The New Code of Canon Law states: 'No one may lawfully
   exorcise the possessed without the special permission of the
   local Ordinary. This permission is to be granted by the local
   Ordinary only to a priest who is endowed with piety, knowledge, prudence and integrity of life' (Canon 1172). When
   a person is obviously possessed the bishop must be
   approached. He must be part of the discernment. For a more

detailed discussion of this point see the book by Cardinal
Suenens, *Renewal and the Powers of Darkness*.

7 Inner Healing and the Sacraments of Reconciliation and Eucharist

1 For further reflections on these sacraments see my book *The Healing Power of the Sacraments*, St Paul's Bombay.
2 Decree on the Ministry and Life of Priests, 5.
3 Constitution on the Sacred Liturgy, 47.
4 The Redeemer of Man, 10.
5 Constitution on the Sacred Liturgy, 47.

8 Praying for Physical Healing

1 Life of Priests, 5
2 For a comprehensive and clear exposition of different ways of praying for people see the excellent book by Fr Benedict Heron OSB, *Praying for Healing: The Challenge*, London 1989.
3 Cf. *Priest and People*, March 1994, p 114
4 Encyclical on Suffering, 14.
5 Ibid.
6 Ibid. 15.
7 Ibid. 26.
8 Ibid. 24.
9 New Rite of Anointing, 5.
10 Ibid., 6.